ABOUT THE AUTHORS

DR. GLORIA PERERA is a senior researcher in Malacology at the Instituto Pedro Kouri in Havana, Cuba. She has been involved in research on freshwater snails of medical importance and especially on the biological control of intermediate snail hosts of parasites in the Caribbean area.

JERRY G. WALLS is a senior biology editor at TFH Publications and the author of over 20 books and 100 articles on various animal groups, including four books on conchology. He also has described almost a dozen species of cones and cowries.

APPLE SNAILS IN THE AQUARIUM

AMPULLARIIDS: THEIR IDENTIFICATION, CARE, AND BREEDING

Dr. Gloria Perera and Jerry G. Walls

ACKNOWLEDGMENTS
Our thanks to the Department of Malacology, Academy of Natural Sciences, Philadelphia (ANSP), for assistance in photographing shells from their collection.

Title page: Pomacea maculata from the Amazon River (ANSP 50671). This was one of the first species of apple snail described by European scientists and also is one of the largest. It often is called *P. gigas*, in error. Photo: W. P. Mara.

Distributed in the UNITED STATES to the Pet Trade by T.F.H. Publications, Inc., One T.F.H. Plaza, Neptune City, NJ 07753; distributed in the UNITED STATES to the Bookstore and Library Trade by National Book Network, Inc. 4720 Boston Way, Lanham MD 20706; in CANADA to the Pet Trade by H & L Pet Supplies Inc., 27 Kingston Crescent, Kitchener, Ontario N2B 2T6; Rolf C. Hagen Inc., 3225 Sartelon St., Laurent-Montreal Quebec H4R 1E8; in CANADA to the Book Trade by Vanwell Publishing Ltd., 1 Northrup Crescent, St. Catharines, Ontario L2M 6P5 ; in ENGLAND by T.F.H. Publications, PO Box 15, Waterlooville PO7 6BQ; in AUSTRALIA AND THE SOUTH PACIFIC by T.F.H. (Australia), Pty. Ltd., Box 149, Brookvale 2100 N.S.W., Australia; in NEW ZEALAND by Brooklands Aquarium Ltd. 5 McGiven Drive, New Plymouth, RD1 New Zealand; in Japan by T.F.H. Publications, Japan—Jiro Tsuda, 10-12-3 Ohjidai, Sakura, Chiba 285, Japan; in SOUTH AFRICA by Lopis (Pty) Ltd., P.O. Box 39127, Booysens, 2016, Johannesburg, South Africa. Published by T.F.H. Publications, Inc.
MANUFACTURED IN THE UNITED STATES OF AMERICA
BY T.F.H. PUBLICATIONS, INC.

TABLE OF CONTENTS

Ventral view of a Golden Apple Snail, *Pomacea bridgesi*. The foot, mouth, and two pairs of tentacles can be seen clearly, while the retracted siphon is barely visible to the side. Photo: E. C. Taylor.

1: THE WORLD OF APPLE SNAILS

APPLE SNAILS IN GENERAL

Despite the attractive colorfulness of the sea world, the freshwater world has its own magic. Water is the very essence of life and is our most precious possession. Freshwater biotopes play a vital role in preservation of nature and the existence of human beings. These magnificent sources of life are...the world of apple snails.

Apple snails or ampullariids often are regarded as insignificant inhabitants of freshwater habitats, but they can be very useful to man in several senses or they can cause trouble if not well manipulated. Additionally, they are popular aquarium pets that are bred and sold in large numbers by both American and Far Eastern breeders, and they are the most popular freshwater aquarium snails.

Many of the freshwater snails are of medical importance since they serve as intermediate hosts for different kinds of parasites that can afflict both man and animals. Schistosomes, a type of fluke or parasitic worm, are the most important parasites that need snails to complete their life cycle, and more than 200 million people in America, Asia, and Africa are infected every year. The only effective method to control these snail-transmitted diseases is by controlling the intermediate host (the snail) so the cycle cannot be completed. This can be achieved by means of chemical substances added to the water (molluscicides) that kill the snails but pollute the water, or by using biological control agents,

Schistosomes, *Schistosoma*, are parasitic flukes related to the gill flukes of fishes. A major scourge of humans throughout the tropics, their larvae *(miracidia)* develop in snails to become cercariae (a type of larva, left). After the cercariae leave the snail intermediate host, they penetrate the skin of humans wading in the water and become adults (a joined pair, right) living in the liver or the bladder. Art: J. R. Quinn.

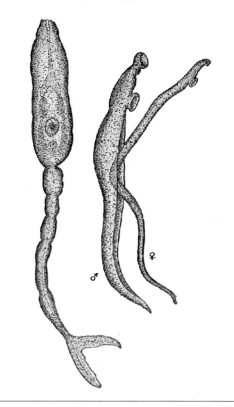

♂ ♀

among which the ampullariids play an important role.

Nematodes of the genus *Angiostrongylus* also can afflict man severely. *Angiostrongylus cantonensis* is a parasite that produces eosinophilic meningoencephalitis and is transmitted by a wide variety of land and freshwater snails, among which there are several species of the genus *Pomacea*. *Pomacea canaliculata*, a Neotropical species that has been introduced into Southeast Asia and currently is spreading over the Oriental area, has been the source of sporadic epidemics due to the ingestion of raw snails. Living apple snails often are sold in Oriental markets and are considered a delicacy worth culturing as a side crop in rice and taro fields. This has caused

Above: The apple snail *Pomacea canaliculata* for sale in an Oriental market in Honolulu. Photo: Dr. R. H. Cowie.

Below: Hawaiian taro patch infested with the apple snail *Pomacea canaliculata*. Notice the many pink egg masses attached to the plants. Photo: Dr. R. H. Cowie.

When introduced into the Orient and Hawaii, American apple snails such as *Pomacea canaliculata* have become nuisances or even serious crop pests in rice and taro fields. The loss of crops often exceeds the gain from edibility of the snails. Photo: Dr. R. H. Cowie.

Apple snails may be the most common invertebrates in the freshwater aquarium. Photo: M. Panzella.

problems when the snails attacked the crops themselves, as they have done in Hawaii.

Ampullariids also are a good choice for use in the aquarium. Several species live well with fishes and can help keep the aquarium free of algae. Others, on the contrary, will eat all the aquatic vegetation since they are voracious herbivores, unless a food supply is provided so as to satisfy their appetite.

Apple snails are the biggest freshwater snails. In the Americas, apple snails commonly are found in tropical rivers, streams, lakes, and ponds. Unlike the wonderfully colored shells of the snails that can be found in the sea, most freshwater snails bear shells that lack the brilliant colors and unusual shapes that encourage shell collectors. Few apple snails are what the average shell collector would call attractive. In general, they have a blackish to tan, globose shell (only one genus, *Marisa*, has a discoidal

or flattened shell, though several African *Lanistes* have depressed shells) with colored bands that vary from olive-green to brownish or yellowish depending on the species. The band patterns and intensity of the color may vary among different populations of the same species, making this group one of the most variable and difficult to classify of all the snails.

WHERE APPLE SNAILS FIT

The phylum Mollusca includes all those animals commonly known as snails, slugs, nudibranchs, oysters, clams, octopuses, and squids. The mollusks are all invertebrates with a soft body (Latin *mollis*, soft) that in most cases (though not always) is protected by a shell. The shells, in all their different shapes, sizes, and colors, have always fascinated people and led to the study and collection of the shells, the science or hobby of conchology. More scientific study of mollusks, including the anatomy of their soft parts, is known as the science of malacology.

Apple snails, like this *Pomacea bridgesi*, are typical freshwater mollusks. Notice the operculum sticking out behind the shell. Photo: E. C. Taylor.

The phylum usually is divided into seven classes, the only one that concerns us being the Gastropoda, the class that includes the marine, land, and freshwater snails. They are asymmetrical in the placement of the internal organs (the organs become twisted in relation to the axis of the animal during development, a process known as torsion), and most have a shell consisting of a single spiral valve (as opposed to clams, the bivalves, with two valves or shells). The abalones and limpets, among others, do not have spiral shells but only a single simple valve; slugs and nudibranchs do not have an external shell at all, either covering the shell with the soft body (mantle) or losing the shell entirely. The head is well-differentiated, with eyes and one or two pairs of tentacles. The foot is well-developed, and in the prosobranchs or gill-breathers (including the apple snails) it carries on the posterior dorsal surface (i.e., behind the shell) a horny or calcareous structure named the operculum that the animal uses to close the mouth or

Apple snails can retract their entire body into the roomy shell and then close it off with an operculum. Photo of *Pomacea bridgesi*: E. C. Taylor.

aperture of the shell when the foot and body are retracted into the shell. Their feeding habits vary from voracious carnivores to herbivores, but omnivores are predominant.

This group is the most important class from the medical standpoint, since most of the mollusks that transmit diseases or are venomous are gastropods. They also are very important economically, because some of them are edible (escargot, conch fritters, etc.) and a few, such as the Queen Conch, even are able to produce very valuable pearls.

Snails generally are divided into three subclasses: the prosobranchs or gill-breathers (which contain the apple snails and many other freshwater snails), the opisthobranchs (including the nudibranchs), and the pulmonates or air-breathers (mostly land snails, but also many small freshwater snails).

Most of what projects from a snail's shell is the foot. The intestines and other organs are always hidden within the shell. Photo of a golden *Pomacea bridgesi*: E. C. Taylor.

CLASSIFICATION OF MOLLUSKS

For many years the mollusks were classified mostly by external characters, most of them found on the shell. This led to great confusion, since the same species when presenting subtle differences due mostly to environmental conditions was described by different authors as different species. This is the main reason that some names have become synonyms. When all the characters of a particular group are reviewed, usually many names are found to be synonyms of only a few species, a situation very familiar in the confused

Because coloration varies so greatly (compare this almost black *Pomacea bridgesi* with previous photos), more stable structures of the shell and internal anatomy must be used in classification. Photo: E. C. Taylor.

taxonomy (study of classification or identification of organisms) of apple snails. To accomplish a good classification, it is important to take into account the different features of both the shell and the animal. Unfortunately, apple snails still have never been thoroughly studied in terms of their anatomy.

Shell

One of the most important characteristics that distinguishes the different species of snails is the shell. (See the glossary at the end of the book for definitions of unfamiliar terms.) The shell is the product of secretions by specialized cells of the mantle, which is a kind of fleshy body enclosure typical of all mollusks. The shell, though homogeneous in appearance, has three different layers. The most external one, the periostracum, is a very thin protein film (conchiolin) that usually is brownish or translucent. The middle and innermost layers are called the ostracum and hipostracum respectively and are composed of calcium carbonate crystals that are oriented perpendicular to the shell surface in the first case and parallel in the second.

Especially useful in identification are the size and shape of the shells. They vary from very small individuals that can be as tiny as a few millimeters in diameter, like a Cuban

Shells coiled to the left (a) are **sinistral**; those coiled to the right (b) are **dextral**. Most apple snails are dextral, but the *Lanistes* species are sinistral. Art: Dr. M. Yong.

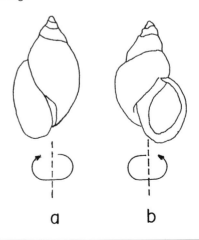

a   b

helicinid land snail that inhabits only the Desembarco del Granma National Park in the easternmost part of Cuba and is the smallest shell in the world, or as big as the Florida Horse Whelk (*Pleuroploca gigantea*), which can attain 2 feet in length. The shell may take various shapes, ranging from very elongate to globose (spherical), patelliform (limpet-like), or discoidal (a coil flattened above and below so everything is in one plane). The coils or whorls of the shell may turn to the right (clockwise, dextral) or to the left (counterclockwise, sinistral). They can be rounded, angular, shouldered, or flattened. Often there is a hole at the base of the shell, the umbilicus, about which the whorls seem to coil; it can be narrow, wide, absent, or even filled in with shelly material. Some groups of snails have shells ornamented with spines and frills and bright colors, while others are very plain in shape and simple in coloration, making them very difficult to separate from only the shell characters.

The shells of freshwater snails can vary greatly in shape. Common forms include: a) elongate; b) globose; c) patelliform; d) turreted; e) discoidal. Art: Dr. M. Yong.

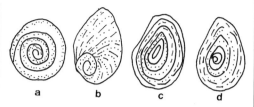

The operculum is sometimes useful in separating species. Common types include: a) multispiral; b) paucispiral; c) concentric; d) concentric with spiral nucleus. Art: Dr. M. Yong.

Operculum

Many snails, especially those that breathe with gills, have special glands that secrete a horny or calcareous operculum, which is a kind of trapdoor that protects the animal from predators or from adverse conditions. The form and shape of the mouth or aperture of the shell and consequently its operculum are important characteristics that can be used to separate the different species of snails. In a few groups the mouth and operculum can be sexually dimorphic in shape, and in the apple snail genus *Pomacea* some males and females can be separated (by an experienced eye) through this character. In a few "live-bearing" species of *Pomacea*, the operculum may have a distinctive ridge indicating the point where the eggs were held before hatching.

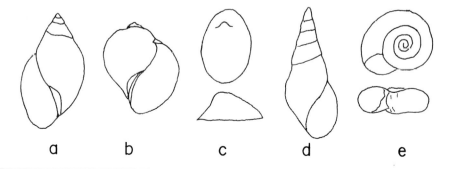

a   b   c   d   e

Radula

In snails, the radula is a rasp-like structure located in the anterior end of the digestive tract (the mouth, in other words) behind the jaws and is used to scrape off food fragments during feeding. The radula has a number of longitudinal and transverse rows of minute teeth that vary in shape and number according to the species. There are three categories that are useful in taxonomy: central,

Radular teeth often are a good criterion for recognizing species. Teeth in different parts of each row have different shapes and names: C) central; L) lateral; I) internal marginal; M) marginal. Art: Dr. M. Yong.

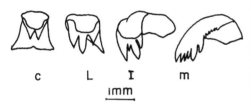

lateral, and marginal teeth. All apple snails (as far as known) have radular teeth in the formula 2:1:1:1:2 (each row of teeth consists of two marginal teeth, one lateral tooth, a central tooth, one lateral tooth, and two marginal teeth). Unfortunately the radular teeth of apple snails are quite variable from individual to individual and are of little taxonomic utility, though the development of the cusps on the teeth has been used as a generic character.

Egg Masses

Oviparous snails such as the apple snails usually lay eggs in clusters whose form and number are somewhat characteristic. Freshwater pulmonate snails such as pond snails lay translucent gelatinous egg masses attached to aquatic plants or other substrates in the water. Many apple snails also lay gelatinous egg masses (the eggs are embedded in a mass of jelly) attached to plants, rocks, or debris near the water surface, as in the case of *Marisa* and *Lanistes*. Others produce clusters of hard-shelled eggs placed outside the water, attached to emergent vegetation, roots, or even the upper edges of aquaria, as is the case in *Pomacea* and *Pila*. The color, shape, and number of eggs in the egg mass may be characteristic of different species, but there is little

A mass of newly laid eggs of an apple snail. Photo: M. P. & C. Piednoir.

If you look closely, you can seen many rows of radular teeth in the open mouth of this *Pomacea bridgesi*. These teeth allow the snail to scrape or rasp algae from glass and flesh from the bones of rotting fish. Photo: E. C. Taylor.

published information on the subject.

Internal Anatomy

The organ systems of mollusks sometimes have characters that separate close species. Often species of the same genus are difficult to separate only by the shell, radula, or operculum due to their similarity. Anatomical features exposed by dissection are especially important to achieve an accurate separation of species in such cases. The reproductive system sometimes offers important anatomical evidence that has led to the current classification of most species of freshwater snails, but so far it has been of limited use in classifying apple snails. The structure of the kidney also seems to be of some use in classification.

Life Tables

Biological and ecological characteristics as well as anatomical structure can be used to define the taxonomic status of a particular species, since reproductive strategies as well as growth patterns and mortality rates may be specific. Life tables are a group of particular characters of the species (reproduction, mortality, growth, and life span) that can be easily determined in nature by means of simple measurements of various shell features. Special software has even been designed to determine the life tables of the species in order to study the ecology of snails, which is important to the understanding of the environment and its preservation. The variation of the life patterns of the species is

The second pair of long tentacles or labial palps that project on each side of the head (the first pair of true or cephalic tentacles project from the base of the eyes) are characteristic of apple snails and help distinguish them from viviparids with similar shells. Photo of *Pomacea bridgesi*: E. C. Taylor.

Shells of snails introduced into Hawaii. Top left, *Cipangopaludina chinensis* (Viviparidae); top right, *Pila conica*; bottom right, *Pomacea bridgesi*; bottom left, *Pomacea canaliculata*; center, *Pomacea paludosa*, juvenile. Photo: Dr. R. H. Cowie.

evident even in related species, as is the case of the Caribbean species of *Pomacea*.

SURVEYING THE FAMILY

The apple snails, family Ampullariidae (also known as the Pilidae), are almost entirely confined to tropical and

subtropical areas. In America the family extends from central Mexico to the La Plata basin, as well as the West Indies and Florida and Georgia. In Africa it extends northward along the Nile into lower Egypt but is most abundant in the central part of the continent. In the Oriental region ampullariids can be found from India and Sri Lanka eastward through Thailand and most of the East Indies (but not New Guinea).

The operculum in apple snails (above and below left) usually is a large, flat plate that rides on the posterior top of the foot. When the foot folds as the animal retracts into the shell, the operculum comes to close the mouth of the shell. Photos of golden *Pomacea bridgesi*: E. C. Taylor.

The mollusks belonging to this family include the largest freshwater snails. The apple snails typically are large and globular or subglobose in shape, although a discoidal form is present in the genus *Marisa*. The shells usually are brown, tan, or blackish and may be banded, with a greenish or brownish

Most apple snails are dark brown to blackish in body color with flecks or mottling of brighter yellow to red pigment. Additionally, most species also bear dark spiral bands on the shell. Photo: M. P. & C. Piednoir.

Steps in siphon extension. Here the siphon is barely visible projecting from alongside the head. Photo: E. C. Taylor.

periostracum. In America the family is represented by the genera *Pomacea*, *Marisa*, and *Asolene*, while in Africa the genera *Pila*, *Lanistes*, *Saulea*, and *Afropomus* are found. Asia has only the genus *Pila*. The species of *Pila* have a hard, calcified operculum, while in the other genera (as far as known) the operculum is horny and somewhat flexible; this distinction often is difficult or impossible to see, however, and many *Pila* have opercula that look like many *Pomacea*. Additionally, *Pila* are hatched with horny opercula and add calcium deposits as they grow.

In the ampullariids the cephalic tentacles (which have the eyes at their bases, sometimes on short stems or

Now the siphon has become a more elongated tube surpassing the eyes. Notice that the siphon is patterned similarly to the body in this specimen of *Pomacea bridgesi*. Photo: E. C. Taylor.

The siphon now extends to the surface of the water, allowing atmospheric air to reach the pulmonary or lung compartment of the snail's body. Most apple snails must breathe air at least occasionally to survive. Photo: E. C. Taylor.

peduncles) are filiform (thread-like) and very long. (The soft anatomy of many apple snails is completely unknown, so we are talking about structure in the well-known genera only.) In addition to the true tentacles there is a pair of labial palps projecting from the snout (to either side of the mouth) that look like an additional pair of tentacles.

The mantle cavity of apple snails is divided into two portions: the right side contains a gill for aquatic respiration, and the left side functions as a lung for aerial respiration. There is a leaf-like appendage on either side of the neck (the nuchal lobes), of which the left one functions as a siphon for air intake. This siphon is very long in *Pomacea* and *Marisa*, short in *Pila*, *Lanistes*, and *Afropomus*, reported as relatively short or

Portrait of a beautiful Golden Apple Snail, *Pomacea bridgesi*. Photo: M. P. & C. Piednoir.

oddly developed in *Asolene*, and unknown in *Saulea* (but probably short). The siphon is very flexible in *Pomacea* and can be contracted or extended as necessary to reach the surface to breathe.

Apple snails have separate sexes, and subtle sexual dimorphism is evident in some species. Males have a short penis (inside a heavy sheath formed from the mantle edge) that is used to transfer sperm to the female; in *Pila* the sperm groove is on the outside of the penis, while in *Pomacea* it is internal. Females of *Pomacea* and *Pila* typically lay egg clusters out of the water on stalks of aquatic or emergent plants, on rocks, bridges, or other hard substrates. The egg clusters vary in form and color and can be white, pink, orange, red, yellow, or green with a hard, calcareous shell. *Marisa*, *Lanistes*, and probably *Asolene* lay shell-less eggs in gelatinous masses submerged in the water.

Apple snails have a fairly long fossil history in the Old World, with specimens assigned to *Lanistes* recorded from the Eocene (37.5-54 million years ago) of Egypt and the Miocene (5-26 million years ago) of Kenya. *Pila* also is known from the African Miocene and within the last million years or so occurred in what is now the Sahara Desert as well as the cold, mountainous areas of northern India.

Lake Hanabanilla in Cuba (left and below) is a locality in which *Pomacea paludosa* and *P. poeyana* are abundant. Photos: Dr. J. P. Pointier.

Grand Etang in Guadeloupe is one of the habitats for *Pomacea glauca* on this Caribbean island. Photo: Dr. J. P. Pointier.

Lake Valencia is an ampullariid habitat in Venezuela. Photo: Dr. J. P. Pointier.

This pond in Guadeloupe was completely covered with water lettuce, *Pistia* (right). After *Pomacea glauca* was introduced, most of the water lettuce was eaten and the pond was revived (below). Photos: Dr. J. P. Pointier.

Grand Etang in Guadeloupe harbored a high density of water lettuce, *Pistia*, that was used as food and refuges by snail hosts (vectors) of schistosomes (right). The aquatic vegetation diminished because of the biological control action of ampullariids (below). Photos: Dr. J. P. Pointier.

Though sexes are separate in most apple snails, they are hard to distinguish externally. The penis of the male is a thickened tubular area at the side of the foot and is not easily seen in living specimens. These are mating pairs of *Pomacea urceus* from Venezuela (above) and *P. haustrum* from Brazil (below). Photos: Dr. J. P. Pointier.

2: BIOLOGY AND ECOLOGY OF APPLE SNAILS

REPRODUCTION

Ampullariids are dioecious; that is, they have separate sexes. In some species the males and females can be identified by the form of the aperture of the shell and the operculum. This is so in the case of *Marisa cornuarietis* and several species of the genus *Pomacea*. There are some species, such as *Pomacea canaliculata*, in which the sexual dimorphism is clearly visible. *Pomacea poeyana* is an example in which the males have the aperture and operculum more rounded than in females. These characters have proved to be statistically significant when compared by sex, and those familiar with the snails can tell them apart easily. Males and females of *Pomacea paludosa*, on the other hand, cannot be separated externally.

Some *Pomacea* and *Pila* can change their sex from male to female. In *Pila* the animal needs a preparatory estivation period, but in *Pomacea* the sex change can occur in either the estivating season or when the animal is active. During the change, the testis becomes rudimentary and changes color.

Females of *Pomacea* and *Pila* lay their eggs out of the water. In the American species the eggs usually are pigmented and are calcareous. The color of the egg masses varies from one species to another, and within some species there is considerable variation in color as well. This is the case in *Pomacea canaliculata* in Argentina, in which the eggs also vary in size from 2.24mm to 3.47mm (representing variation both between and within populations). Females of some species can spawn repeatedly without any new contact with males. This is the case in *Marisa*

Diagram of the reproductive system of *Pomacea poeyana* from Cuba. Pp, penis pouch; P, penis; Shc, sheath channel; Psh, penis sheath; Pr, prostate; Sp, sperm duct; T, testis. Art: Dr. M. Yong.

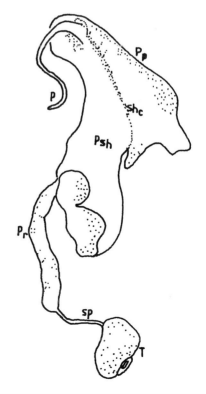

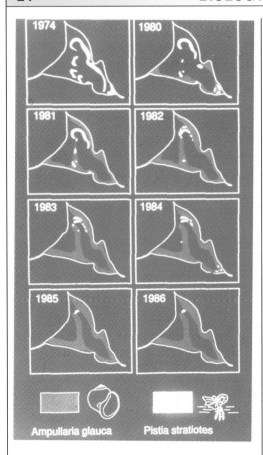

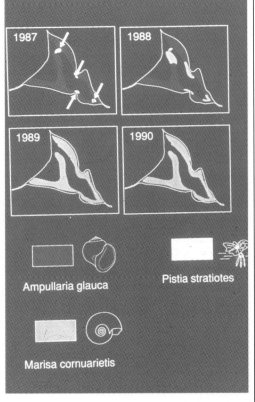

Left: Relationship between populations of *Pistia* (water lettuce) and *Pomacea glauca* in Grand Etang, Guadeloupe, over a 12-year period. Above: Reduction of aquatic vegetation in Grand Etang by *Pomacea glauca* and *Marisa cornuarietis*. Art: Dr. J. P. Pointier.

cornuarietis, Pomacea paludosa, and *Pomacea canaliculata.*

As for reproduction, there are two types of egg clutches in *Pomacea* species. The most common one is the type of cluster deposited out of the water in keeping with the amphibious habits of the parent, which have a siphon for aerial respiration in addition to a gill for aquatic respiration. The egg masses are attached to emergent vegetation, bridges, or any other hard surfaces available. In Cuba, oviposition of both *Pomacea paludosa* and *Pomacea poeyana* is observed during the whole year, with reproductive peaks that usually appear in months when

El Rubio Lake, Cuba, holds a dense population of *Pomacea paludosa.* Photo: Dr. J. P. Pointier.

The feeding action of *Pomacea glauca* is intense, and they are able to eat a great amount of aquatic vegetation each day. Photo: Dr. J. P. Pointier.

An egg mass of *Pomacea falconensis* on the stems of aquatic vegetation in Venezuela. Photo: Dr. J. P. Pointier.

An egg mass of *Pomacea poeyana* in Lake Hanabanilla, Cuba. Photo: Dr. J. P. Pointier.

Empty egg shells from a *Pomacea poeyana* egg mass in Lake Hanabanilla, Cuba. Photo: Dr. J. P. Pointier.

the temperature is at its lowest. The other mode is one observed in species that live in temporary ponds or seasonally dry water bodies. These animals lay a few giant eggs that are brooded in an incubation chamber under the shell between the operculum and the aperture. This is the case in *Pomacea urceus*, which lays orange eggs loosely attached to each other and to the inner surface of the shell. This attachment to the female's shell results in egg scars that are permanent. Development of the eggs occurs during the dry season. The crawling young remain under the female's shell until the start of the rainy season.

The genus *Asolene* lays its eggs under the water in a gelatinous mass, at least according to a few limited and perhaps questionable

Recently laid egg masses of *Pomacea poeyana* in Lake Hanabanilla, Cuba. Photo: Dr. J. P. Pointier.

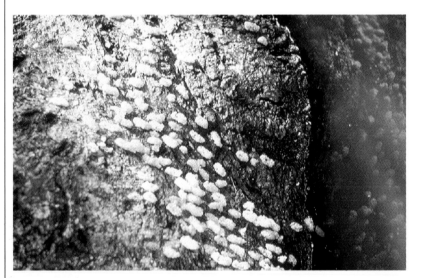

Rocks protruding from the water are a good oviposition site for *Pomacea glauca* in Guadeloupe. Photo: Dr. J. P. Pointier.

Pomacea glauca laying eggs on stems of emergent vegetation in Guadeloupe. Photo: Dr. J. P. Pointier.

observations. These snails do not have a well-developed siphon.

FEEDING HABITS

Ampullariids have three main types of feeding habits. They usually are herbivores and feed on macrophytes (green leafy plants). They also can be scavengers; several species have been observed feeding on dead fishes. Some ampullariids can feed on microscopic organisms by browsing or ciliary feeding. Most of the *Pomacea* and *Pila* species are vegetarians. Damage to rice paddies and taro fields has been reported from many Asian countries and from Hawaii, often leading to laws restricting the sale and distribution of apple snails in the aquarium and food markets.

Marisa cornuarietis is a very voracious snail that eats vegetation without selectivity,

Numerous egg masses of *Pomacea paludosa* in Canasi, Cuba. Photo: Dr. G. Perera.

taking any plants that become available and also scavenging. This habit led to the assumption that the snail would make a good biological control agent for other snails transmitting diseases, since they eat the egg masses of the intermediate hosts as well as new-born snails.

Pomacea paludosa lays eggs on whatever substrate is available out of the water. These egg masses are deposited on emergent vegetation in Lake Hanabanilla. Photo: Dr. G. Perera.

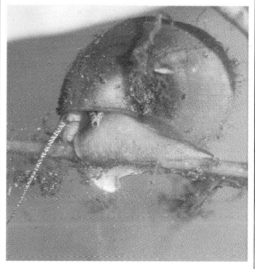

Pomacea glauca crawling on aquatic vegetation and showing the cephalic tentacles. Photo: Dr. J. P. Pointier.

Pomacea glauca is a heavy feeder. It can be observed here eating water hyacinths, *Eichhornia*. Photo: Dr. J. P. Pointier.

Biomphalaria glabrata is the main intermediate host of schistosomiasis in the Neotropical region, where the disease is endemic in most countries. Photo: Dr. J. P. Pointier.

Unfortunately, but perhaps predictably, it was found that *Marisa* becomes a pest in rice paddies.

Since the early 1950's, apple snails have been used as biological control agents of other snails. *Marisa* was first used in Puerto Rico and has been observed feeding on egg masses, young, and even adults of *Biomphalaria glabrata*, the snail intermediate host for schistosomiasis in America. After 20 years of study of the use of ampullariids as biological

Schistosome-bearing snails can be very abundant in some water bodies, but their abundance can be diminished by the introduction of ampullariids. Photo of *Biomphalaria glabrata*: Dr. J. P. Pointier.

controls, a great reduction in the biomphalarid populations was observed. The Dominican Republic also experienced similar results. A few years after the introduction of *Marisa* into the northern and central parts of the country, the intermediate host snail was displaced from its

A sieve is a useful tool when collecting ampullariids in aquatic vegetation. Photo: Dr. G. Perera.

original habitat.

Pomacea glauca is another of the species that has been used as a biological control agent because of its voracious appetite for vegetation. Grand Etang, Guadeloupe, is a natural lake in the mountains about 400m above sea level near the volcano La Souffriere. It held a dense population of the intermediate host of schistosomiasis capable of transmitting the disease. This ampullariid was introduced to the lake and began eating the water lettuce (*Pistia*) that covered most of the surface of the lake and served as both food and a home for the intermediate host snails. Little by little the host snails were reduced in numbers and eventually disappeared.

COLLECTING AMPULLARIIDS

Collecting tropical freshwater snails could be a very interesting hobby, as freshwaters are a unique environment. There are places that can be surveyed safely because there are no dangerous animals or risks of infection, as are most rivers and lakes in southern North America and Cuba. The same cannot be said for water bodies in Africa or South America, and even some West Indian islands have regions infested with snails that spread schistosome larvae and can infect any humans wading in the water. In those areas the collector needs to be careful and must wear the appropriate gear such as boots and gloves and should use long-handled nets.

Ampullariids usually are found

Above: Ampullariids are found on the aquatic vegetation, where they can be hand-picked while feeding. Photo: Dr. G. Perera.

feeding in the vegetation. Some of the more unusual forms are found attached to rocks in the rapids of rivers.

After collecting the snails, they can be kept out of the water for a few days (remember, most are air-breathers), but they must be kept moist to stay alive. The best way to carry them is to put them in plastic boxes with damp paper towels on the bottom and a few holes in the lids to let in air. The snails also can be carried by wiping their shells dry and wrapping them in newspaper. A paper bag will be good enough to keep in moisture and let in air. After arriving at

Below: The irrigation channels of watercress beds are a good site to collect apple snails. They often can be found in high densities. These are the best places to collect them for human consumption. Photo: Dr. G. Perera.

An adult Snail Kite, *Rostrhamus sociabilis*, displays the dark coloration and bright red eye typical of the species. They are a major predator on apple snails in the Neotropics.

Caiman Lizards, *Dracaena guianensis*, are strange aquatic relatives of the Tegu. They feed almost exclusively on apple snails and have teeth that are heavy, rounded knobs to better crush snail shells. Because of their dependency on snails as food, they seldom do well in captivity. Photos: K. H. Switak.

their destination, the snails should be revived by putting them in dechlorinated water at a temperature similar to that in their natural habitat.

ENEMIES

Ampullariids have many enemies. The most important one is man, as they are used for food in many countries. They also are sought by handicrafters because of the interest of their shells. Some birds prey heavily upon them, including the Snail Kite, a major predator from southern

Left: This juvenile Snail Kite clearly displays the slender but strongly hooked bill developed by the bird to pierce the bodies of apple snails.

Below: Limpkins, *Aramus guarauna*, are large brown wading birds found from Florida and Georgia south to Argentina. Their range parallels that of the apple snails, the preferred food. Photo: M. Walls.

The left-overs of a Snail Kite feast at El Rubio Lake, Cuba.

Florida through the Antilles and tropical America, and the Limpkin, a large wading bird with a similar distribution. The odd caiman lizards, *Dracaena*, of South America (close relatives of the tegus) feed almost exclusively on *Pomacea*.

BREEDING AMPULLARIIDS

Probably most of the ampullariids can be raised in aquaria, though there is little real experience in these endeavors. For those ampullariids with marked amphibious characters, the aquarium should be provided with a ramp making it easier for them to reach the air, and they may need a soft bottom in which to estivate before reproducing.

Dirty water should be filtered and replaced with clean water at regular intervals; these snails do not tolerate dirty water and are very sensitive to their own wastes. The snails have to be handled gently during water changes or they could die.

They can be fed different kinds of vegetables (lettuce being pretty good), aquatic plants, or even paper. As a food source, aquatic plants such as *Elodea*, *Cabomba*, *Lemna*, and other plants with soft leaves are excellent. Fish food flakes provide a good supplement to their diet. We'll discuss keeping and breeding common apple snails more fully in the next chapter.

3: APPLE SNAILS IN THE AQUARIUM

Once upon a time, apple snails were simply large dark brown or blackish snails that ate fish food, aquarium plants, lettuce, algae, and occasionally fish eggs in the aquarium. Today, however, the hobbyist has a greater choice of more attractive snails to be found in any pet shop. They come in several colors and sizes, and you even have some selection as to how voracious your pet will be.

APPLE SNAIL OR MYSTERY SNAIL?

First, let's try to get rid of a bit of confusion over common names. All the species of *Pomacea* technically are apple snails regardless of their size or color. Unfortunately, however, dealers today often use the name "apple snail" strictly for large, usually brownish species such as *Pomacea maculata* or for the United States native species *Pomacea paludosa*, which is wild-collected in Florida. The somewhat smaller and often brightly colored *Pomacea bridgesi* usually is called a "mystery snail" today. The reason for this divergence of names is rather complicated and dates back to the early history of the aquarium hobby.

For many years after the turn of the century, hobbyists in America used locally collected snails in their aquaria. In the northeastern United States, where most aquarists were until the 1930's, the largest local snails were the fairly large (up to 50-mm or so), olive brown, round-shelled *Viviparus* and *Cipangopaludina* from local lakes and ditches. These snails belong to the family Viviparidae, give live birth to numerous tiny duplicates of the parent, and have been known as mystery snails in the English literature for almost two centuries.

Sometime in the 1930's, the first *Pomacea* species began to appear in the pet shops, probably most as casual imports or contaminants of the rare fish shipments arriving from South America into the German and United States markets. These

Though apple snails long have been popular in aquaria, they only become truly common with the development of golden varieties. Photo: W. P. Mara.

were mostly small, brown, round-bodied species (often called by the probably incorrect name *Ampullaria cuprinus* in the older literature) that looked much like the more familiar viviparids. In fact, most hobbyists probably would find the shells of the two groups of snails almost identical at first glance and wouldn't bother noticing the differences in the animals. (We'll mention these differences later when we talk a little bit about viviparids.) The two taxonomically very different types of snails became confused in the hobby books and magazines and in the minds of both aquarists and dealers.

When tropical fishes began to

A Golden Apple Snail, *Pomacea bridgesi*, with its siphon well-extended. Photo: E. C. Taylor.

be raised in large numbers in ponds in southern Florida, dealers quickly found that imported tropical *Pomacea* lived well in the ponds with the fishes and even laid eggs (usually infertile). Most hobbyists by now were heating their water instead of keeping it at room temperature, and the tropical snails filled a niche in the market for an oddball that could take warm water (viviparids prefer it cool). In a few years some dealers were breeding apple snails in quantity, marketing them under both that name and as mystery snails, a name more familiar to older hobbyists.

By at least the late 1960's, *Pomacea bridgesi* seems to have become the dominant apple snail on the American market, though larger Brazilian species occasionally made their way into aquaria and some dealers still collected wild *Pomacea paludosa* in South Florida canals. Then a mutation occurred in *Pomacea bridgesi* that eliminated most of the greenish pigments from the shell and body, and dealers had a hot new sales item, a bright golden yellow 50-mm (2-inch) snail. This morph or variety was marketed as the "albino mystery snail" (aquarists always love albinos), and a new aquarium animal was born. Of course all the *P. bridgesi*, of any color, then began to be marketed as mystery snails, while any other species entered the lists as apple snails. Some dealers are still confused and call every snail that's big and round a mystery snail, including

Though normally colored apple snails are interesting animals, their brown colors would not appeal to most hobbyists. Photo of *Pomacea bridgesi*: W. P. Mara.

the occasional viviparids that show up in pet shops. The names thus have come full circle.

BASIC KEEPING

Taking care of an apple snail is simple. As long as you give them clean, warm water, access to the air, and sufficient food, they will do fine for at least a few months. The water should be at least neutral and preferably basic (alkaline), which is a good rule of thumb when keeping any snail. Remember that snail shells are calcium compounds bonded to a living organic membrane, and acid water dissolves calcium compounds. In nature few snails of any size live in strongly acid or black waters, and those that do tend to have very pitted, eroded shells that are thin and fragile. Apple snails and Cardinal Tetras, for instance, do not mix for very long. Apple snails are fairly tolerant of moderately soft, neutral water and will even survive in water of a pH as low as 6.7 or so, but pH 7 to 8 is best. Try to provide about ten hours of light per day.

Though apple snails have both a gill and a siphon for breathing atmospheric air, most specimens seem to prefer living near the surface of the water, often climbing up the glass or plants to the water-air interface. If you do not allow the snail access to air

Varieties of the common apple snail, *Pomacea bridgesi*: White animal with white (translucent) shell. The dark upper whorls are due to the liver and other internal organs showing through the shell. Photo: E. C. Taylor.

Varieties of *Pomacea bridgesi*: White animal with golden shell. Photo: E. C. Taylor.

(as by filling the aquarium all the way up to a tight-fitting coverglass or lid), it will be uncomfortable and might very well die from lack of oxygen. Play it safe and let it breathe.

Water temperatures in the 70's are sufficient for apple snails, and they usually will survive for a while at lower temperatures. In nature they often inhabit shallow waters that may reach 100°F for short periods, but of course such extremes are not recommended in the aquarium. They are not especially sensitive to light because in nature they feed on green aquatic plants, often in shallow water and at the surface. They will burrow in soft substrates, however, especially when they follow the natural cycle of trying to estivate in the mud during the dry season.

Few hobbyists have much luck keeping apple snails for more than a year or so (there are exceptions, of course) or breeding them. This possibly is because they don't have facilities to let the snails estivate each year. In nature many apple snails seem to live at least three or four years (with records approaching the decade mark), but at least four months of each year may be spent buried in the mud, inactive and barely alive. Growth and breeding resume with the coming of wet season rains. It seems possible that if an apple snail is kept constantly active in warm, wet surroundings, it simply burns out.

FEEDING

Apple snails are, as we have seen, herbivores. They eat almost any green plant they can get their jaws around. Certainly if they can eliminate the water hyacinths and *Pistia* from entire Caribbean lakes, they have the ability to eat all the plants you might put in their aquarium. You can keep apple snails and plants together, however, by keeping the snails

heavily fed on lettuce, elodea, fish food flakes and pellets (veggie based), boiled peas, carrots, and most other vegetables and fruits. A snail will tend to eat soft plants first, the ones that are easier to chew.

There is a persistent aquarist belief that different apple snails have different feeding habits. It is widely believed, and possibly correct, that *Pomacea paludosa*, the wild Florida snails, will devour all vegetation in the aquarium, whether soft-textured or hard and calcareous. *Pomacea bridgesi*, on the other hand, is thought to attack hard plants only after all soft plants have been eaten; if you give it plenty of elodea it won't attack the more valuable plants. Remember that common knowledge sometimes is more common than knowledgeable; whether you want to risk expensive plants is a decision you have to make yourself.

Though they prefer leafy plants,

Though apple snails are not especially sensitive to pH, it is best to keep them in neutral to alkaline water to avoid excessive shell erosion. Your local pet shop will have a variety of pH test kits and solutions to adjust the pH in your aquarium. Photo courtesy Aquarium Pharmaceuticals.

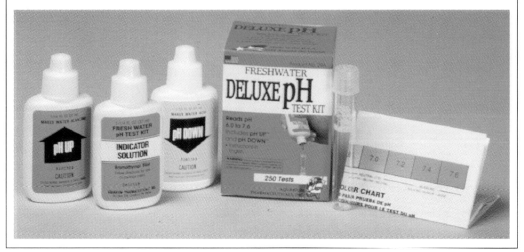

apple snails also will eat large quantities of algae if it is available. They prefer filamentous types but if necessary will scrape encrusting algae of various types from the aquarium glass. Though not especially fond of diatoms and similar unicellular algae, they will do quite well in green water for at least a while. It is best to not stress a snail and force it to eat an inferior diet, however. Give it a varied, abundant diet just as you would a fish.

WASTE

Did you ever dissolve an infusoria tablet in a quart of water and put it in the sunlight to grow paramecia, elodea, and green water to fed to young fishes? Before tablets and cultures became easily available, aquarists used snails, especially apple snails, as a source of infusoria base. In fact, apple snails once were widely called infusoria snails.

Apple snails are big eaters and they produce a lot of waste. Think of them as palm-sized lawn mowers without a mulching bag attached to the side. The waste has to go somewhere, and it goes into the aquarium water. Keeping several adult apple snails in a small aquarium requires heavy filtration and special attention to water quality. If you are keeping fishes with the snails, be especially careful: snails can go to the top and breathe air, but fishes are stuck with what they can get from the water. The more waste in the water, the less oxygen will be available to the animals.

Speaking of fishes, one last caveat. Though apple snails are vegetarians, they are not beyond scavenging on occasion. A small, sleeping fish can look almost as tasty as a small, dead fish to a hungry snail, so be careful, count your small fishes often (or keep them in a tank separate from the snails) just to be alert for a "rogue killer" snail, and make sure the snails are well-fed at all times. By the way, fish eggs are great food for almost any type of snail, basically a tasty, yummy snack food. Breeding fishes and snails do not mix; don't even try it.

SOME APPLE SNAIL VARIETIES

The bright golden yellow "albino mystery snail" certainly is the most popular apple snail. Little has been written on this color morph, but it probably was just a spontaneous mutation that was seized upon by a Florida

Small aquarium setups are excellent for keeping a few apple snails without competition from fishes. Remember that there must be access to atmospheric air, however, for the snails to thrive. Photo courtesy Hagen.

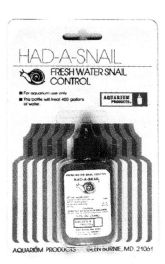

Small snail species often go out of control in the aquarium and must be eradicated by means of chemicals when other control methods fail. Photo courtesy Aquarium Products.

breeder. Today they are bred both in Florida and the Far East and shipped to aquaria around the world. These basically seem to be some type of unstable albino or xanthic color form. The greenish brown pigments are missing or nearly so, allowing the underlying yellow pigments to show through. If you look closely at the shell of one of these snails, you often will see traces of the brownish lines found on normal *Pomacea bridgesi.* The animal typically is almost colorless with bright yellow to orange spots and bands of pigment (especially around the eye) instead of the blackish brown or tan with black spots typical of the species. There seem to be variations between fully albinistic (colorless animal, translucent white shell), xanthic (the foot yellowish and the shell distinctly yellow to brownish), and almost fully pigmented snails.

Normal shells of *P. bridgesi* are pale to medium brown with a strong greenish tinge. They have a variable pattern of narrow brown lines over the shell, and the mouth or aperture may be dark brown. The lines may be abundant and narrowly spaced or few and widely spaced; some shells may lack lines over most or all of the shell. The body usually is dark brown with a somewhat translucent greenish sheen. There may be darker blotches over the top of the foot.

Less often seen than albinos or normals are melanistics. Melanistics often appear slaty blue overall rather than the greenish brown of normal snails.

It is not impossible that environmental constraints such as water quality, temperature, and amount and type of food during the early developmental stages may have an influence on color. In natural populations of some apple snails such

During the winter months you may need to heat the snail aquarium. A good aquarium heater should be all you need to keep your snail pets warm and contented. Photo courtesy Hagen.

Although *Pomacea bridgesi* is the most commonly sold apple snail, other species do appear in the hobby on occasion. One of these is a large, sometimes bright yellowish species with a dark animal. Sometimes sold as "the" mystery snail or the Inca snail, these fist-sized animals perhaps represent *Pomacea maculata*. *Pomacea canaliculata*, with deep channels between the sutures of the spire whorls, also is a large brown species to be looked for in the aquarium trade. Photos: E. C. Taylor.

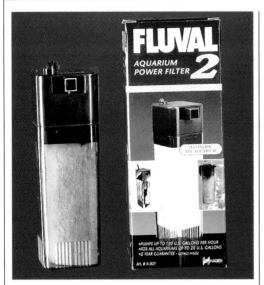

Apple snails are dirty animals, so either you must do a water change every day (very inconvenient) or you have to purchase a high-quality power filter to keep the tank clean. Photo courtesy Hagen.

constraints produce larger or smaller shells of thicker or thinner shell texture and with or without patterns. There is a lot of room for controlled breeding experiments with apple snails and manipulations of their environment while the snails are still babies.

BREEDING

As you already have read, apple snails usually lay round, hard-shelled eggs in large clusters attached to plants and rocks or debris at or just above the edge of the water. Typically they hatch out while there still is water in the lake or canal, and the baby snails simply fall into the water and crawl away. Apple snails often lay clusters of pink, white, or even green eggs at the edges of the aquarium, and they have been known to fall out of tanks while

Varieties of *Pomacea bridgesi*. Top: White (translucent) shell, black animal (plus a giant Inca snail for size comparison). Middle: The wild type, with a striped brown shell and a blackish animal. Bottom: A striped brown shell with a white animal. Photos: E. C. Taylor.

Varieties of *Pomacea bridgesi*. Top left, golden shell, white animal. Top right, white (translucent) shell, white animal.
Middle left, dark striped shell and blackish animal. Middle right, white (translucent) shell, white animal.
Bottom left, white (translucent) shell, whitish animal. Bottom right, white (translucent) shell, black animal. All photos: E. C. Taylor.

Varieties of *Pomacea bridgesi*. Top left, white (translucent) shell and black animal. Top right, brown-striped shell and white animal. Bottom left, white (translucent) shell, black animal. Photos: E. C. Taylor.

looking for egg-laying sites. Many of the eggs laid in captivity fail to develop and assumedly are infertile.

Sexes are separate but are not externally distinguishable in apple snails unless you have a practiced eye and can detect the somewhat narrower and more vertical shell mouths of males as compared to females of some species. Egg-laying just seems to happen in the aquarium, but it is more common in outdoor ponds and the large vats used by some commercial breeders. Soft bottoms seem to help, since these snails are used to such bottoms and retreat into them to estivate.

Basically, for commercial

Commercial apple snail culture in Florida is a simple process. The adult snails are made comfortable in large concrete vats in a greenhouse (above) and fed on scrap lettuce and green water. Eventually the mature females leave the water and lay their egg masses attached to the sides of the vats above the water level (below). Photos: E. C. Taylor.

Close-up of egg masses of *Pomacea bridgesi* on the side of a concrete vat. Photo: E. C. Taylor.

The hardened egg masses are scraped off the sides of the vats and transferred to a piece of screening over a fresh vat of water. As the eggs hatch, the little snails drop through the mesh and fall into the water below. The snails just are allowed to grow to salable size in the vat. Photo: E. C. Taylor.

breeding several fully grown snails are put into a large tank of some type, preferably with a soft bottom of sand. Mating "happens," and the female proceeds to lay one or several clusters of eggs on canes, sticks, or pieces of wood suspended at the edge of the tank. Breeders then remove the egg clusters to a separate vat or pond for better control. The egg clusters are placed on a large-mesh screen and allowed to dry in the shade. Interestingly, the bright colors of the eggs often fade to white after a week or two. The young hatch in a few weeks (often three) and fall or crawl into the water, where they may feed for a while and then retreat into the bottom to wait out a dry season of lowered water levels.

Obviously such conditions are difficult to produce in the average home aquarium, but some aquarists have successfully bred *Pomacea bridgesi* and even the large *P. maculata* on occasion. Even if the egg clusters turn out to be infertile, the bright pink to pale red (*P. bridgesi*), pearly white (*P. paludosa*), or even green (*P. glauca, P. maculata*) eggs are certain to be a conversation piece in the aquarium room. Persistence and luck may win out in the end.

Harald Schultz's classic photo of bright pink egg masses of a species of *Pomacea* from Porto Alegre, southeastern Brazil.

4: AMERICAN APPLE SNAILS

In the Americas there are three generally recognized genera of ampullariids, though the southernmost forms of the genus *Asolene* are so variable that they sometimes have been broken into three full genera. (Remember the glossary at the back of the book if you have trouble with technical terms.)

Pomacea Perry, 1810

This genus contains species with rather thin, more or less globose shells with ovate apertures. The umbilicus typically is open and distinct, though in the subgenus *Limnopomus* the umbilicus may be reduced or absent (imperforate). The eggs usually are laid outside the water, have a calcareous shell, and vary in color and size according to the species. The siphon is long and very extensible, the animals being amphibious.

The species inhabit rivers, streams, lakes, and canals, and also can be found in swamps, ditches, and pools with abundant aquatic vegetation. The taxonomy is very confused, with most workers recognizing between 75 and 150 very variable species, though there are indications that many fewer species are valid. All the species are difficult to identify, and few are likely to ever be encountered by the casual naturalist or aquarist. The following list is therefore just a sampling of the genus.

Most American Apple Snails belong to the genus *Pomacea,* but a few southern species are placed in the poorly defined genus *Asolene.* Photo: W. P. Mara.

Pomacea paludosa, the Florida Apple Snail, is a big ampullariid common to the southern United States and Cuba. Photo: Dr. J.P. Pointier.

Albino and pigmented shells of *Pomacea paludosa* from El Rubio Lake, Cuba. Photo: Dr. J. P. Pointier.

Remember that it takes more than a large shell to make an apple snail. Notice the absence of labial palps (the second pair of tentacles) on the head of this unidentified snail. It probably is a large viviparid rather than an apple snail. Photo: A. Spreinat.

Pomacea paludosa (Say). This species, the largest freshwater snail of Florida and Cuba (typically 40-70mm high in adults), commonly is known as the Florida Apple Snail. The shell usually is thin, with a rather low spire that may be variable depending on the environmental conditions and a more or less rounded shoulder on the body whorl. It is greenish to brownish in color with darker spiral bands; a thick-shelled,

reddish brown form has been named *miamiensis* but is of uncertain status. The interior of the mouth sometimes is violaceous, and the dark bands are visible from the inside of the shell. The aperture flares somewhat anteriorly and is weakly constricted posteriorly. Although extremely unusual, a sinistral specimen was reported from Florida. The species occurs over all the Florida peninsula but westward only to the Suwannee and Choctawhatchee Rivers. It also is found in the Ocmulgee and Flint Rivers in Georgia, but low winter temperatures prevent it from inhabiting northernmost Florida.

It is an edible mollusk that is consumed locally in several areas, though it can be the intermediate host of a dangerous nematode, the rat lungworm (*Angiostrongylus cantonensis*); they must be well-cooked. Specimens often are collected for the aquarium trade from the wild in Florida. This species has a reputation for devouring aquarium plants, however. It seems to prefer deeper waters and is very common in artificial lakes, where it attains high densities. It has been observed that in lakes on the Isle of Pines, Cuba, they are able to live and keep stable populations in waters that are relatively acid (pH 5.5) due to the presence of rotting pine needles. There are fossil records from the Pliocene (1 to 13 million years ago) of Florida.

Pomacea poeyana crawling on the bottom of a shallow pool in Lake Hanabanilla, Cuba. Photo: Dr. G. Perera.

Pomacea poeyana (Pilsbry). The shell of this Cuban species is medium to large in size (about 40mm), solid and strong, with an abruptly conical, low spire and a widely open umbilicus. The suture is very deeply impressed, with the following whorl rising above it. The color is variable, but it is predominantly whitish with a cream periostracum and numerous dark bands that vary in width and usually are brownish. The aperture is oval and the lip is strongly expanded, with a pale yellow border, the upper margin rounded. Sexual dimorphism is evident and can be observed in the shape of the aperture and operculum and overall size (more rounded in the smaller male). It is commonly found in shallow waters with muddy bottoms, such as rice paddies and watercress beds.

Pomacea haustrum (Reeve). The shell is medium to large in size (about 50mm) and relatively thin. The spire is subelevated and

Pomacea haustrum from Brazil. Photo: Dr. J. P. Pointier.

the whorls are well-rounded. The suture is deep, mostly in the body whorl. The color is variable, with brownish predominant and multiple spiral bands that vary from narrow to wide. The aperture is wide and ovate. Sometimes the thin, horny operculum is smaller than the aperture and does not

Another view of Pomacea poeyana. Photo: Dr. G. Perera.

Views of *Pomacea lineata* (ANSP 220772) from Lago Baptista, Brazil. Photos: W. P. Mara.

close it tightly. The species is common in artificial lakes in Brazil and occurs throughout the Amazon River region westward to Bolivia and Peru and southward into the Paraguay River and southeastern Brazil.

Pomacea lineata (Spix). This large (30 to over 80mm), globose species is moderately heavy. It is horn brown in color with darker brown spiral bands. The apex is subelevated, with four or five rounded whorls that increase rapidly in diameter and are separated by deep sutures. The aperture is large and ovoid. The outer lip is sharp, and the umbilicus is narrow and deep. It is found in rivers, canals, and ditches in Atlantic drainages of

Brazil from Para State to Rio de Janeiro.

Pomacea glauca (Linnaeus). This exceedingly variable species may be quite small to large (about 70mm) and also varies considerably in shape. Typically it is somewhat globose and moderately thick, but many varieties are distinctly depressed, with the spire not projecting much beyond the rounded body whorl. (There is a strong possibility that *Marisa* is derived from a species much like this one.) The anterior lip flares widely and the inner edge (the columella) is thick and glossy. The color also varies, and the species can be found from a pale yellow with brown spiral bands to a brownish yellow or purplish color with darker spiral bands that are evident on the inside of the shell as well. The colorful variety *gevesensis* from Guyana has a solid white mouth without banding, a reddish columella, and bright brown banding against a very pale background; the umbilicus is widely open. This species is found in the Dominican Republic, Lesser Antilles, and northern South America from Colombia and Venezuela through the Guianas and perhaps south into the Amazon (the synonymy is very confused). It inhabits clean, clear water, including flowing streams, canals, ditches, and (especially) lakes, where it can reach high densities as in Grand Etang, Guadeloupe, and Lake Valencia, Venezuela. The eggs are bright green and about the size of a small pea. *P. glauca* occasionally

Variation in the shells of *Pomacea glauca* from Venezuela and (upper middle) Guadeloupe. Photos: Dr. J. P. Pointier.

appears in the aquarium trade but seldom is common; it sometimes is bred in captivity.

Pomacea urceus (Mueller). This very large species (some specimens have measured 115mm in height) is very variable, and specimens vary in shape from very globose to slightly elongate; the spire is low, the whorls rounded and weakly shouldered. The lip is greatly expanded in most specimens and may be bright red. The color usually is blackish to brownish or even yellowish with darker brown bands, but typically specimens are covered with a heavy, dark, rough periostracum. The umbilicus is wide.

Currently most authors consider *P. nobilis* (Reeve, 1856) to be a synonym of *P. guyanensis* (Lamarck, 1819) and *guyanensis* to be a synonym of *P. urceus*. Typical *urceus* seems to be the

Pomacea urceus from Venezuela. Photo: Dr. J. P. Pointier.

Pomacea urceus (ANSP 120273) from Pebas, Peru. Photo: W. P. Mara.

form found in flowing, relatively clear, permanent waters of forested areas, while the *nobilis/guyanensis* form is more typical of still or stagnant backwaters and swamps of savannahs. Typical *P. urceus* is more globose than typical *nobilis/guyanensis*, which is somewhat more pear-shaped and often lacks the rough periostracum of typical *urceus*. The two types appear to not be found together.

Egg clusters of this species vary from orange to pale green (perhaps another indication of multiple species within this name). They are placed between the undersurface of the operculum and the aperture of the female when she estivates after the mating season. A sinistral specimen was recorded from Venezuela. The species may estivate over 8 inches deep in the mud.

P. urceus is found from northwestern South America through the Guianas and into the Amazon basin west to Peru. Only the *nobilis/guyanensis* form seems to be found in the Amazon basin, but both it and typical *urceus* are found in the Guianas. Another related species, subspecies, or ecotype, *P. urceus olivacea* (Spix), is found in swampy forests of the Rio Negro to Manaus; it has a narrow, sometimes closed umbilicus and typically lacks banding under the relatively thin, pale periostracum.

Pomacea sordida (Swainson). This is a large (86mm), globose

Pomacea sordida (ANSP 120305) from Rio de la Plata. Photo: W. P. Mara.

shell with greenish or horn-colored periostracum and dark spiral bands. The apex is subelevated, and the shell presents four or five moderately shouldered whorls that increase rapidly and are separated by a deep suture. The aperture is large, moderately round, yellowish or violaceous. The lip is thick and the umbilicus is deep. It is found in ditches and streams in Brazil.

Pomacea flagellata (Say). This moderately large (about 50mm) species has the usual subglobose shell and a brownish to greenish brown shell with darker spiral bands. The spire is somewhat flattened at the sides and low, and the umbilicus is narrow and deep. The aperture is narrow above, usually attached far down the side of the body whorl, and rounded and weakly flared anteriorly with a pale orange lip.

This is a very variable species through its range from central Mexico to the Rio Magdalena system of Colombia. One revision recognized four subspecies and over 30 synonyms of this common species. In the typical *P. f. flagellata* (found throughout the range) the periostracum varies from olive-green to reddish brown and color bands may be seen over the entire shell and through the aperture (or they may be absent). Typical specimens are about 60mm high and almost equally wide. Malleation (the appearance of being hammered or dimpled) is common in this species. *P. f. livescens* (Reeve) is found in southern Mexico and northern

Views of *Pomacea flagellata* (ANSP 120211) from Cartagena, Colombia. Photos: W. P. Mara.

Guatemala and commonly was called *ghiesbrechti* in older literature. It is nearly globular, often almost 100mm high but distinctly narrower, and has a tremendous aperture. *P. f. erogata* (Fisher & Crosse) is a dwarf form (often only 35mm high when fully adult) found in swamps and temporary ponds throughout the range of the typical subspecies, while *P. f. dysoni* (Hanley) is a bright reddish brown shell with a dull orange lip that is supposed to be from Honduras but apparently is not known well enough to be sure even where it comes from. Obviously these subspecies do not agree with modern interpretations of the subspecific concept, and the species remains poorly understood.

Pomacea falconensis Pain & Arias. This medium to large (about 55mm) apple snail is thin and oblong-globose in shape. The

Pomacea falconensis from Venezuela. Photo: Dr. J. P. Pointier.

spire is somewhat elevated, with an acute apex. The first whorls are round, slanting, and the last one is convex, smooth, and covered with a thin pale green periostracum. The shell is reddish brown in color with brown bands of variable width on the body whorl. The aperture is oval and somewhat oblique,

Pomacea canaliculata (ANSP 85067) from Rio Grande do Sul, Brazil. Photo: W. P. Mara.

the operculum is somewhat eccentric near the nucleus, and the umbilicus is narrow and deep. It is reported only from Apurito Island in Venezuela.

Pomacea canaliculata (Lamarck). Variable in size from small to moderate (30 to 55mm), the shell is brownish with darker spiral bands visible from the inside of the thin shell. The spire is subelevated and the aperture is wide. The sutures between the whorls are very deep (i.e., canaliculate), giving the shell an

Operculum (above) and top view (below) of *Pomacea canaliculata* (ANSP 85067) from Rio Grande do Sul, Brazil. Photos: W. P. Mara.

odd appearance when viewed from the apex. Shells often are malleated or dimpled.

This species exhibits sexual dimorphism involving the shapes of the aperture and operculum, whose relative widths are significantly different in the sexes. Males have a narrower mouth than females and also have a heavier shell than females. There is a record of a sinistral (left-handed) female specimen from Argentina. When kept in an aquarium with two dextral (normal or right-handed) males, they were observed mating but no spawning occurred, possibly due

to inversion of the organs in the visceral mass (i.e., the penis and vagina were on the wrong sides to permit successful sperm transfer). This is one of the most ubiquitous species of South America, where it is found from Colombia and the Guianas to Argentina. It has been introduced into several Asian countries as a food crop and now is found in Japan, Thailand, Hawaii, and even Australia. It also has been recorded from extreme southern Texas, possibly the result of escapes from the aquarium hobby. Specimens sometimes are found in the aquarium trade, where they have

been called Giant Inca Snails, among other names, and small numbers seem to be bred commercially in Florida with *P. bridgesi*, the more common aquarium apple snail or Mystery Snail.

Pomacea bridgesi (Reeve). This is the common apple snail, the Albino Mystery Snail or Golden Mystery Snail, of the aquarium hobby. The whorls of the spire are distinctly stepped, leading to a rather sharp or acute apex or point. The shoulders of the whorls are nearly flat, and they are separated by deep sutures. Typical adults seldom exceed

Top view of a wild *Pomacea bridgesi* (ANSP 120303) from Bolivia. Photo: W. P. Mara.

Pomacea bridgesi (ANSP 120303) from Bolivia. Photo: W. P. Mara.

50mm (the species varies from 40mm to about 65mm in height). The wild coloration is greenish tan with numerous narrow and wide bright brown bands over the shell, these often visible through the mouth. The umbilicus is narrow but deep, and the aperture is flared anteriorly and somewhat narrowed posteriorly, being attached rather low on the body whorl.

The actual name and relationships of the common aquarium apple snail are somewhat doubtful because it and its relatives in South America are poorly understood. True or typical *bridgesi* was described from Beni in Bolivia and is rare and virtually unknown; it is a large shell, over 65mm high, and has the top of the body whorl and aperture very wide and shelf-like. The form in the hobby apparently

corresponds to *P. b. diffusa* Blume, a smaller (average height under 40mm), darker form with a less shelf-like top of the body whorl and aperture. It is widely distributed through the Brazilian and Peruvian Amazon but also was described from Bolivia. Also to be considered in this mix of names is *P. aulanieri* (Hupe & Deville) from the Peruvian Amazon, a form with a very wide aperture and short spire.

All seem to be related to *P. scalaris* (d'Orbigny), the oldest name of the group, which is a more southern form found from Uruguay and Argentina north into southern Brazil and Bolivia. This is a large species (ranging from 50mm to over 70mm high) with a very flattened body whorl that often has a strong ridge or carina on its surface. The spire is high and pointed, and there may be many malleations on the shell surface. There are indications that its eggs are not like those of *P.*

An old *Pomacea bridgesi* showing evidence of healed scars and severe breaks in its shell.

Pomacea aulanieri (ANSP 120471) from Maranon, Peru. Photos: W. P. Mara.

bridgesi, being softer, and the similarity in shell shapes may be superficial.

We discussed variation in *P. bridgesi* in the chapter on apple snails in the aquarium. Suffice to say that it is a typical *Pomacea* in its biology, laying reddish eggs and estivating in the mud during the dry season.

Other Species

It would be foolish to try to list all the other described *Pomacea* in a book for aquarists, but a few other species deserve a quick mention.

Pomacea vexillum variety (ANSP 8190) supposedly from Venezuela. Photos: W. P. Mara.

One of the oldest names in the apple snails, **P. maculata** Perry, often is seen in the aquarium literature under the synonym P. *gigas* (Spix). This is probably the largest known freshwater snail, with specimens over 155mm high and 135mm wide being recorded. It has a thin, fragile, brownish shell with a very wide aperture. Like other thin, large apple snails, it usually is found in still, deep waters with dense vegetation. Rubber collectors are reported to have used it to collect wild latex, and it occasionally appears in the aquarium hobby.

P. papyracea (Spix) is known as the Papershell Apple Snail or Exploding Apple Snail because the shell is so thin and fragile that

Pomacea maculata (ANSP 50671) from the Amazon River, operculum above. Photos: W. P. Mara.

when it dries the heavy periostracum literally pulls the underlying shell apart, making it very hard to collect nice

Pomacea maculata (ANSP 50671) from the Amazon River. Photo: W. P. Mara.

specimens. Young specimen are almost black, while full adults (to over 110mm high) may be bright reddish brown with a white aperture. There never are any bands on the shell. The Papershell is widely distributed over northern South America from Venezuela and the Guianas through the Amazon basin, living in quiet swamps where it may bury itself almost a foot deep in the mud during the dry season. It is said to be a favorite prey of the Snail Kite, which pierces a specimen behind the operculum with its sharp bill and then waits until the injured snail releases its grip on the operculum and lets the bird gain access to the soft body parts.

Pomacea insularum (d'Orbigny) is a large (often over 100mm high and 110mm wide), low-spired species with a gigantic, almost round aperture. The color usually is brownish, with weakly defined darker bands. This species has an unusual shell sculpture, the fine vertical (axial) growth lines of the shell being crossed with narrow longitudinal lines. This is a southern South American species typical of swamps and slow rivers in savannahs from southern Brazil,

A specimen drawer full of large, broken Papershell Apple Snails, *Pomacea papyracea*, from Brazil in the Academy of Natural Sciences, Philadelphia. Most of the damage is natural, caused by stress from drying periostracum on the thin shell. Photo: W. P. Mara.

including the Mato Grosso, into Argentina and Uruguay. It appears to be related to the more northern *lineata*, but admittedly all these species are poorly understood.

Finally, a few words about some of the species of the subgenus or genus **Limnopomus**. These are relatively small, thick-shelled species that tend to have the umbilicus very narrow or actually filled in with shelly material (imperforate). They often have a very granular texture or sculpture to the shell, a feature shared with *Asolene (Pomella)* from southern South America. These are species of swift, often rocky, waters from northern South America to Peru. At one time they were placed in the genus *Asolene*, but today they usually are considered to be odd *Pomacea* but probably worth ranking as a full genus. If reports that it lays non-calcareous eggs under rocks in water are correct, it certainly would deserve generic status.

P. (L.) sinamarina (Brugiere). The shell is thick and varies from olive-green with brown bands to uniformly dark brown. The aperture is convex. The eggs are reported to be laid during the dry season on the undersurface of rocks in rapids where the snails live. The species is found in river rapids in Guyana, attached to rocks where the current is most violent. **P. (L.) granulosa** (Sowerby) has the shell extremely variable, from thick with a low spire to thin with a medium high spire. The color generally is olive-

green with brown spiral bands. The umbilicus usually is narrow and the aperture convex. It can be found in the calm zones of rapid rivers or on their shores. It is found in the northwestern part of South America living with *Pomacea urceus*. **P. (L.) crassa** (Swainson) is a medium to large shell (about 50mm) with a rather high spire. The color of the shell varies from greenish yellow with brown spiral bands to a uniform dark brown. There is no umbilicus. The aperture is convex. This species prefers small rivers and creeks at a depth that

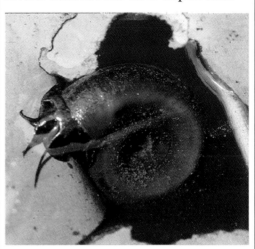

Marisa cornuarietis, often called the Colombian or Giant Ramshorn, is a voracious feeder on most aquatic plants. Photo: Dr. J. P. Pointier.

rarely surpasses 2 feet. They live attached to rocks under the falls, where the water is highly oxygenated. The type species of the subgenus is **P. (L.) columellaris** (Gould).

Marisa Gray, 1821

This genus probably comprises only one species, *Marisa*

Marisa cornuarietis is the only American ampullariid with a flattened, discoidal shell. Photo: Dr. J. P. Pointier.

cornuarietis (Linnaeus). The shell is medium in size (35mm to 50mm in diameter), discoidal or flattened, dextral, and has a large, very open umbilicus. The shells of females are larger than those of males, which have the aperture more rounded compared to the relatively narrower mouth with a broadly angulated or truncated outer lip in the female. They have a corneous and concentric operculum. The shell is pale golden brown with bright, sometimes reddish, bands. The eggs are covered with a gelatinous substance and are deposited in the water, attached to plants or floating. They are unusual in being bright orange when first laid, the color disappearing as the eggs mature.

This species is native to South America (particularly Venezuela) but has spread all over the world and today is considered to be a nearly cosmopolitan species. It has been introduced to several countries (including Florida in the United States) by aquarists because of the beauty of its shell, which has attractive color bands. It adapts to a wide variety of habitats such as rivers, lakes, artificial ponds, and irrigation canals with abundant aquatic vegetation.

Usually only the one species is recognized, but there are several others described in the literature that might eventually be assigned species status. The most different may be *Marisa planogyra* Pilsbry, a smaller shell (about 30mm in diameter and 12mm high) with a deeply concave spire and somewhat more tightly coiled whorls. Young shells of this form

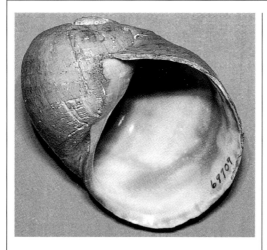

Asolene (Pomella) megastoma var. *neritoides* (ANSP 69709) from San Gabriel's I., off Colonia, Uruguay. At middle is a view of the outside of the operculum, at the bottom a view of the underside of the operculum. Photos: W. P. Mara.

visible from the front, and the whole shell appears thin and fragile though actually quite thick. It is brownish, rough, somewhat granular in sculpture, and sometimes marked with weak brown bands; the lips of the mouth are glossy white, the mouth itself often violet. It is known only from the Rio Uruguay system. *A. (P.) americanista* (Ihering) is a smaller species (about 60mm high and almost as wide) in which the spire is low but quite visible and the shell does not appear as depressed above as in *megastoma*. It seems to be known only from the vicinity of Iguazu Falls on the Rio Parana.

The three species of **Asolene (Felipponea)** are thick, rather conically oval or globose shells with low, eroded spires and a reduced umbilicus. *A. (F.) elongata* (Dall) from the Rio Uruguay is about 25mm to 30mm high and has the umbilicus developed as a narrow chink, while in the other species the umbilicus is more open. *A. (F.) neritiniformis* (Dall) is a uniformly brown, almost oval shell with the spire heavily eroded and the aperture very large; it may reach over 45mm in height. Seemingly restricted to the Rio Uruguay, it is known from the Dept. Paysandu, Uruguay, in the lower reaches of the river. More to the north, in Rio Grande do Sul, Brazil, it seems to be replaced by *A. (F.) iheringi* Pilsbry, which is a bit more conical, smaller (about 25mm high), and streaked with reddish brown on a yellowish tan background, the lip brightly

Above and below: *Asolene (Pomella) americanista* (ANSP 251769) from the Rio Iguazu between Brazil and Argentina. The operculum is show below. Photos: W. P. Mara.

Above: *Asolene (Felipponea) elongata* (ANSP 141212) from Dept. Paysandu, Uruguay. Photo: W. P. Mara.

striped with brown.

Very little is reported on the natural history of these southern apple snails, and there probably are some surprises waiting for any hobbyist who manages to obtain and keep some of the species. Most of the species of *Asolene* resemble marine snails known as nerites, thick, often colorful little snails of the intertidal and shallow flats that are favored by many collectors of seashells. They are quite different from any of the apple snails, of course, in many details, including a thick operculum with a pair of odd pegs on the sides, but they seem to be adapted to similar environments and able to take turbulent water that would destroy thinner shells.

species, but they remain very poorly studied except in the major lakes and near more populated areas. The size of the shells can vary from medium to very large. All the species are dextral, with convex non-angular whorls. The operculum of this genus has an inner calcareous layer that differentiates them from their relatives with corneous or horny opercula, but the snails are hatched with horny opercula and add calcium deposits as they grow. The eggs are laid in clusters out of the water and have brittle calcareous shells. The siphon is short, as in all the Old World apple snails as far as known. The Asian apple snails are all members of the genus *Pila*. The species of this genus are amphibious, and their respiration may be branchial (by gill) or pulmonary (by lung) depending on whether they are in or out of the water. They breed immediately after they come to the surface after a long period of estivation. The rain seems to be the factor that stimulates their activity, and when the rainy season begins they rapidly increase their populations.

They play an important role as intermediate hosts of parasitic diseases that afflict man. The most important ones are *Angiostrongylus cantonensis* (a nematode that causes eosinophilic meningoencephalitis when the snails are eaten raw or poorly cooked, often resulting in death) and *Echinostoma ilocanum* (a trematode that lives attached to the wall of the small intestine and causes inflammation, ulceration, diarrhea, and anemia in human hosts).

In addition to the native Asian ampullariids, there have been some introductions of American species to Southeast Asia as a source of food or for the aquarium trade. These snails are causing serious damage to rice crops in Taiwan, Japan, the Philippines, China, Vietnam, Thailand, Indonesia, and New Guinea. Three species of *Pomacea* have been introduced to Hawaii from the United States and Southeast Asia (brought in for the food and aquarium trades) and some are now attacking taro crops. In 1981, *Pomacea canaliculata* was brought to Japan for food, but farming of the snails did not become very popular for various economic reasons. The damage caused to rice plants by the feeding snails became a major problem, however. Natural infections with *Angiostrongylus cantonensis* were confirmed in snails collected in several places on Okinawa and the Ishigaki Islands.

A reminder to those who would try local native cuisines in the tropics: **ampullariids must never be eaten raw**, and if just pickled they must be thoroughly impregnated and held in the fluid for a sufficient time to kill any parasites.

African *Pila*

Pila africana (Martens). The shell is medium to large (about 50mm) with strong spiral sculpture. This species inhabits

Pila congoensis (ANSP 131966, Paratype) from Stanleyville, Congo. Operculum above. Photos: W. P. Mara.

small, shaded forest streams under mats of drifted vegetation from Liberia to Ghana and also is common in Zaire and Sierra Leone.

Pila cecillei (Philippi). The shell is large (about 70mm) with strongly convex whorls and is almost shouldered near the suture. It commonly is found in a wide variety of water bodies from swamps to rice paddies and rivers in Madagascar.

Pila occidentalis (Mousson). The shell is medium in size (about 40mm), thin, and fragile. It is pale with narrow chestnut-brown bands. This species lives in Angola, Namibia, and Botswana.

Pila ovata (Olivier). This is a large species (about 115mm) with a variable spire that can be high or low. The operculum is relatively broad. The egg clusters are deposited among stones or in crevices in the substrate. Commonly found in temporary ponds or swamps, it is very abundant on the stony beaches of Lake Victoria. Living snails have been reported from the isolated Siwa Oasis in Egypt, and it can be found from the delta region of Egypt through Kenya and East Africa to Mozambique.

Pila wernei (Philippi). The shell is very large (about 125mm), the largest species of freshwater African snail. The spire is rather short and the aperture is relatively narrow, as is the operculum. Although rare, sinistral specimens have been found. It is common in Somalia and Kenya.

Pila speciosa (Philippi).

Another large species (about 105mm), the shell is globose and rather depressed. The whorls are strongly convex below the suture. Specimens with dark brown bands often are found. This is another species from eastern Africa, including Somalia and Kenya.

Asian *Pila*

Many very similar species of *Pila* have been described from Southeast Asia, where they occur abundantly from Burma and Laos through Indonesia and the Philippines, but not in New Guinea and associated islands. Presently their taxonomy is impossible, and the following species all are taken from recent reports on Thai species.

Pila ampullacea (Linnaeus). This species is large (86mm), brown or olive-green, and rarely

Pila ampullacea (ANSP 388812) from Perlis State, Malaysia. Photo: W. P. Mara.

banded. It is moderately thick and globosely or widely conic, with a low conical or obliquely flat spire. The body whorl is well rounded or evenly convex. The aperture is oval and obliquely rounded near the basal lip. The lip is sharp, thick, strong, and whitish in color. The operculum is thick and heavy, with the inner surface shiny pinkish white. A species of ditches, swamps, and irrigation canals in Thailand, it likes slow-moving water. Specimens are most common from July through October, estivating the rest of the year as much as 3 feet deep in dried mud. They can estivate for at least one year without coming to harm.

Pila pesmei (Morelet). The shell is very variable in size, from 30mm to over 60mm. It is brown, chestnut-brown, or greenish brown with narrow and wide darker spiral bands. This species is thick and globose or wide conical, with a low spire. The early (nuclear) whorls of the spire often are eroded. Four or five whorls usually are present, and the body whorl is well-rounded. The operculum is thick, with a silvery pinkish white nacre. The umbilicus is narrow and somewhat deep. Another species of slow-moving canals, swamps, and ditches, it is common from central Thailand north and tolerates quite polluted water. Most abundant in Thailand from October through December, it can estivate for at least one year.

Pila angelica (Annandale). The shell is large (75mm), chestnut-brown or greenish brown with

Another specimen of *Pila ampullacea* from Perlis State, Malaysia (ANSP 388812). *Pila* and all the other apple snails are notoriously variable in shape and often color. Photo: W. P. Mara.

thin darker brown spiral bands, and widely globose with a low, flat spire. The nuclear whorls usually are eroded. The shell is thin (thicker when the animal is extremely large) and has four whorls; the body whorl has a narrow, smooth shoulder. The aperture is elongately oval, the lip is sharp, thin, and moderately strong, and there is a thin and narrow parietal callus. The color varies from yellowish orange to grayish orange. The operculum is thin, with a steel-blue nacre. The umbilicus is somewhat narrow. This species prefers deeper waters, both standing and moving, where it is found attached to aquatic plants, and is most common (in Thailand) from April to August. It is found from southern Thailand south.

Pila polita (Deshayes). Glossy and moderately thick, this is a large species (about 85mm). It is chestnut-brown or greenish brown in color without spiral bands. The shell is oval to subglobosely conical with a moderately high conical spire. Six whorls are present, and the body whorl is evenly convex. The aperture is oval, the parietal callus thin and wide. The lip is sharp and thin but strong, with an orange or purplish orange tint. The operculum is relatively thin, with a steel-blue nacre on the inner surface. The umbilicus is very narrow and usually is covered by the inner lip. Found in irrigation canals, swamps, and ditches where the water does not flow rapidly, it is most common from March through June, the Thai dry season. This species has proved difficult to keep in captivity because it dies if completely covered with water. It is common from central Thailand north.

Pila gracilis (ANSP 388794) from Selangor State, Malaysia. Photo: W. P. Mara.

Pila gracilis (Lea). This species is a medium to large (about 46mm) shell that varies from ovate-conical to subglobose, the spire subelevated. The nuclear whorls usually are eroded. The body whorl is rounded, the aperture is oval, and the lip is sharp and thin but strong, with a yellow tint. The operculum is thin, with the inner surface nacre steel-blue. The umbilicus is narrow. The shell is chestnut-brown or greenish brown with darker brown spiral bands. This species is found in many types of shallow

Pila gracilis (ANSP 388794) from Selangor State, Malaysia. Photo: W. P. Mara.

Operculum of *Pila gracilis*. Photo: W. P. Mara.

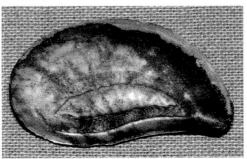

standing waters from southern Thailand south and tolerates pollution well. It is most common in Thailand from April through August. Somewhat surprisingly, it could not estivate more than seven months in the laboratory.

Pila globosa (Swainson) is the common apple snail of India and is one of about a dozen species commonly recognized from that area. Unfortunately, there is little easily available literature on the shells of India and Sri Lanka, and they also are never exported for the aquarium hobby. Like the common species from Thailand described above, most are 30mm to 60mm high, globose or nearly

Pila globosa (ANSP 120355). Photos: W. P. Mara.

Pila conica (ANSP 85083) from Singapore.
Photo: W. P. Mara.

so, with short spires and large mouths. The relationships of the Indian species to the Thai species has proved difficult to establish by traditional taxonomic methods, and the anatomy of the various species has been poorly studied.

Lanistes Montfort, 1810

The shells of this genus are sinistral (i.e., the mouth is on your left as you look at it), but the animals are dextral (that is, their internal organs are in the same positions as in typical apple snails, not twisted to match the shell). The many species have shells that vary from subglobose to ovate or somewhat flattened or discoidal, and the whorls are smoothly rounded, angular, or carinate. The operculum in this genus is completely corneous, as in all the apple snails but *Pila.*

Egg masses are deposited in the water attached to vegetation and lack calareous shells. There are well over 20 species in the genus, but as usual they are poorly known.

Lanistes alexandri (Bourguignat). The shell is small (about 20mm), with carinated spiral whorls and without spiral sculpture or only weak sculpture. It is from Tanzania.

Lanistes bicarinatus Germain. Medium in size (about 40mm), the shell is globose with two carinations, the upper one separated from the suture by a sloping flattened surface. The

Lanistes bicarinatus (ANSP 133874) from Leopoldville, Congo. Photo: W. P. Mara.

umbilicus is surrounded by an angular ridge. The shell is chestnut with darker spiral bands. It is found in Zaire.

Lanistes carinatus (Olivier). A medium (about 40mm) species that is subglobose to ovate and

Lanistes bicarinatus (ANSP 133874) from Leopoldville, Congo. Photo: W. P. Mara.

Lanistes carinatus (ANSP 290067) from the Egyptian Nile. Photo: W. P. Mara.

broader than high. It has one angular carina around the umbilicus and another on the periphery of the body whorl. The shell is brownish with darker brown spiral bands. A species of small ponds or temporary water bodies, it is found from the delta region of Egypt south through the Sudan, Ethiopia, and Somalia to Kenya and Uganda.

Lanistes ciliatus Martens. The early whorls of this medium-sized shell (about 32mm) are strongly carinate and the body whorl is angular. The umbilicus is large and surrounded by an angular ridge. The spire is strongly sculptured with transverse ridges. It is found in seasonal water bodies in Kenya.

Lanistes carinatus (ANSP 290067) from the Egyptian Nile. Photo: W. P. Mara.

Lanistes congicus Boettger. The shell is medium in size (about 40mm), globose, but rather depressed. A strong carination is present near the sutures of the spire and becomes weaker on the body whorl. The surface between the carination and the suture is

Lanistes congicus (ANSP 146195) from Senzala (=Dorf), near Elaw, Congo. Photo: W. P. Mara.

flattened and horizontal. The shell may be banded with dark spiral bands. Common in the Congo, Angola, and Zaire, where it often is found with *Lanistes bicarinatus*.

Lanistes ellipticus Martens. The shell is large (about 50mm), with a medium-high spire and rounded whorls. The umbilicus is wide and angulated. The shell is marked with fine transverse ridges and is brownish green in color. It is found in clear, flowing water on fine gravel from Zaire to southeastern Africa, including

Lanistes congicus (ANSP 146195) from Senzala (=Dorf), near Elaw, Congo. Photo: W. P. Mara.

Mozambique.

Lanistes farleri Craven. In this medium-sized species (about 32mm), the spire is rather high and the whorls are shouldered. The shell is ornamented with spiral ridges. It is brownish with darker spiral bands on the body whorl that are visible from the interior of the shell. Tanzania is its home.

Above and right (operculum): *Lanistes graueri* (ANSP 134008) from Stanleyville, Congo. Photos: W. P. Mara.

Lanistes graueri Thiele. A medium-sized (about 24mm) shell that is thick and smooth, it is strongly angular, with a broad white columellar margin. The spire is elevated. The shell may have dark spiral bands. It comes from Zaire.

Lanistes intortus Martens. This species is medium to small (under 30mm) in size and globose with convex whorls. The umbilicus is angulated. This is a brackish water species sometimes found living with marine mollusks.

Below and right: *Lanistes intortus* (ANSP 221671) from Lolodorf, Cameroons. Photos: W. P. Mara.

Lanistes libycus (ANSP 124622) from the Gabon River. Photo: W. P. Mara.

Lanistes libycus (ANSP 124622) from the Gabon River. Photo: W. P. Mara.

Lanistes libycus (Morelet). This is a medium-large species (about 45 to 55mm) that is globose in shape and more or less carinated below the suture. There is an angulation around the umbilicus. Spiral sculpture is present and usually is strong, with rows of angular periostracum flaps sometimes visible. The shell is yellowish brown and can present darker spiral bands. This is a species of small forest

Detail of the umbilical carina of *Lanistes libycus*. Photo: W. P. Mara.

streams near the coast of Gabon and the Ivory Coast northward.

Lanistes nasutus Mandahl-Barth. The shell is medium in size (about 37mm), fragile, with a very low spire. The body whorl is very expanded and rises above the apex. The aperture, which is higher than the body whorl, has a spout-like basal margin. The umbilicus is surrounded by a strong angulation. Endemic to Lake Malawi, it has been dredged at depths to 90m.

Lanistes neavei Melvill & Standen. This small to medium-sized shell (about 25mm) has a relatively elevated and rounded spire. The shell is pale, with darker spiral bands that can be narrow or wide. It is found in temporary ponds in Zaire.

Lanistes nsendweensis (Dupuys & Putzeys). A small (about 25mm) species that usually is strongly angulated. The spire is relatively high and shouldered, and there are narrow and wide spiral bands marking the shell. Swampy places and streams in forests in Central Africa and Zaire are its habitat.

Lanistes nsendweensis (ANSP 131940) from Stanleyville, Congo. Photo: W. P. Mara.

Lanistes nyassanus Dohrn. This large (about 75mm), thick shell with a very low spire and large aperture has the body whorl rounded and the umbilicus not angulated. A Lake Malawi

Living specimen of Lanistes nyassanus from Lake Malawi. Photo: M. Smith.

Lanistes nsendweensis (ANSP 131940) from Stanleyville, Congo. Photo: W. P. Mara.

endemic, it often is used as a retreat by various cichlids.

Lanistes solidus Smith. Another medium-sized (about 40mm), thick-shelled species with evenly curved whorls. The aperture is large and the umbilicus widely open. The shell is brown and rarely banded. This species inhabits shallow pools in

Living *Lanistes nyassanus* in Lake Malawi. Photo: Dr. W. E. Burgess.

a rather low spire with rounded whorls, in this species the umbilicus is narrow and somewhat angulated. Transverse ribs are present on the shell, which is brownish and unbanded. Another Lake Malawi endemic.

Lanistes stuhlmanni Martens. This is a rather small (about 25mm) species that is thick and slightly carinated. The spire is subelevated and the whorls rounded. It is common in Tanzania.

Lanistes varicus (Mueller). The size of the shell varies from large (about 65mm) to medium (about 35mm), and it is subglobose with

Lanistes varicus (ANSP 120397) from West Africa. Photo: W. P. Mara.

Lanistes varicus (ANSP 120397) from West Africa. Photo: W. P. Mara.

Above and below: *Lanistes adansoni* (ANSP 131950) from San Antonio, mouth of the Congo River. Photos: W. P. Mara.

the rivers of Ghana, Mali, Upper Volta, and Niger.

Afropomus Pilsbry & Bequaert, 1927

This monotypic genus in known only from western Africa. In its single species, *Afropomus balanoidea* (Gould), the shell is rather small (about 20mm), globose, and heavy. The aperture margin is thick and closes the umbilicus; the operculum is corneous. The shell is chestnut-brown with darker spiral bands. A species of small water bodies in Liberia and Sierra Leone, it remains virtually unknown as a living animal.

Saulea Gray, 1861

This is another monotypic genus. *Saulea vitrea* (Born) is a thin, medium-sized (about 45mm) shell with a heavy periostracum.

The spire is rather high, and the first whorls are strongly carinated with spiral rows of hairy periostracum. The operculum is entirely corneous and the umbilicus is narrow. Color and pattern vary greatly, but it is one of the most colorful of an otherwise dull family. There may be dark and light brown bands over the shcll as well as rows of white cloudy markings. A species of western Africa (Liberia and Sierra Leone), it is found in small bodies of water.

Above (operculum) and below: *Afropomus balanoidea* (ANSP 50719) from Cape Palmas, Liberia. Photos: W. P. Mara.

Above and below: *Saulea vitrea* (ANSP 124606). Photos: W. P. Mara.

A variety of African *Pila* species in the collection of the Academy of Natural Sciences, Philadelphia. Museums such as the Academy serve to preserve literally hundreds of thousands of shell and fluid-preserved specimens for use in scientific studies. Many of the unusual apple snails occasionally seen in the hobby can only by identified by detailed comparisons with specimens preserved in museums around the world. Photo: W. P. Mara.

6: OTHER AQUARIUM SNAILS

Compared to the apple snails, the other freshwater snails found in tropical aquaria are insignificant. Few of the literally thousands of tropical snail species have been introduced to the hobby over the years, probably for three major reasons: most freshwater snails are just brownish and not very attractive; many are avid destroyers of aquarium plants and disturb the bottom too much; and many carry potentially dangerous parasites that could become established in humans. For many years there was a tradition of keeping snails from cool northern waters in the aquarium, and some of the established temperate types popular in the 1930's are still around today. There have been almost no significant additions to the aquarium snails other than apple snails for half a century.

Here we will briefly discuss a few snails from six families that appear on a more or less regular basis in pet shops. Some are excellent pets but all have disadvantages of various types. The families we'll discuss are the Viviparidae, the Lymnaeidae, the Planorbidae, the Physidae, the Thiaridae, and the Neritidae.

VIVIPARIDS

At first glance the viviparids or live-bearing mystery snails look like small apple snails. In fact, the family Viviparidae is closely related to the Ampullariidae, differing in several features of the anatomy but having very similar

Viviparids or true mystery snails are easily collected in cooler areas. Though not colorful, they are unusual in giving birth to fully developed young and they are easy to care for. Photo of *Cipangopaludina chinensis*: J. A. Cavalier.

Left: A pond snail, *Lymnaea* sp., and its egg cluster. There are many almost identical species of pond snails, and they are not uncommon contaminants of elodea and other water plants that are sold in pet shops. They are harmless, interesting animals if not allowed to multiply to excess.

shells. Viviparids are fairly large, often almost 50mm high, globose or nearly so, but with large, distinct spires and rather small mouths compared to apple snails. The Japanese Mystery Snail, *Cipangopaludina japonica*, is the largest species, reaching a full 50mm in height; it has a distinct carina on the whorls and the spire is tall and narrow. The very similar Chinese Mystery Snail, *C. chinensis*, averages a bit smaller and has a somewhat lower and broader spire; it lacks the carina on the whorls of its relative. The natural history of the Chinese Mystery Snail is fairly well known. Young are born during the warm summer and early autumn months and grow rapidly, feeding on diatoms, algae, and other detritus in the bottom. Females are mature at an age of one year and continue to produce young

Below: The common native viviparids of the eastern United States are species of *Campeloma*. This is a female *C. decisum* from New Jersey. Notice that there are only two tentacles, not four as in apple snails. Photo: M. & J. Walls.

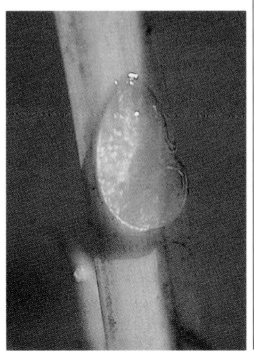

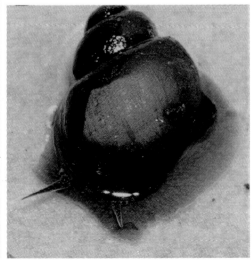

Campeloma decisum (and other viviparids) has a truly gigantic foot that often appears notched at the front center. These snails do well in small aquaria, where they feed on algae and detritus of various types. The clusters of white eggs, by the way, are those of the smaller tadpole snail *Physella*. *Campeloma* gives live birth and in most of its range is parthenogenetic, lacking males. Photos: M. & J. Walls.

Ramshorns are common snails in most freshwaters, but most are too small to excite the aquarist. These probably are a species of *Gyralus* from northeastern North America. The reddish color of ramshorns is fairly distinctive. Photo: J. A. Cavalier.

until they die at about five years of age. Males are smaller than females and shorter lived, usually dying by the age of three years. Though not colorful (they tend to be rather bright olive-green overall), they are easy to keep in water that is not much above 75°F (24°C); they cease to feed and eventually die at continuously higher temperatures.

More likely to be collected in lakes and ponds than purchased in the pet shop are species of the genera *Viviparus* and *Campeloma* in the United States. *Viviparus georgianus* is an attractive snail about 35mm high and quite inflated; four bright chestnut bands form an attractive pattern on the tan body whorl. Several species of *Campeloma* and its close relative *Lioplax* are native to eastern American streams and lakes and are easily collected. They unfortunately are dull tan to simple olive-green in color and usually just 20mm to 30mm long.

The family Viviparidae differs from most apple snails in having the umbilicus reduced to a narrow chink or slit or entirely covered. The animals are quite different, lacking the long tentacles on either side of the mouth typical of apple snails and also lacking a long siphon. They breathe through a gill. Additionally, male viviparids usually have the right tentacle enlarged and curved, serving as a sheath to house the penis. Some *Campeloma* are parthenogenetic, lacking males in many or most populations. Most viviparids give birth to from ten to 30 young at a time.

Keep viviparids relatively cool and feed them on the usual green plants, algae, and sometimes dead fish and other detritus. Some viviparids are voracious foragers on soft plants, and others have a reputation for attacking fish eggs.

LYMNAEIDS

The pond snails form the family Lymnaeidae, an air-breathing group typical of the temperate or even cold waters of the Northern Hemisphere though with members in most freshwaters of the world. Most species are small, well under 25mm, but the great pond snails, genus *Radix*, may reach 60mm in height. Most are fairly simple and typical snails in appearance, generally brown or blackish, with tall, pointed spires, wide to narrow apertures with thin lips, and normal dextral shells. The animal is not exciting, but the tentacles are flattened and triangular rather than conical or thread-like as in almost all

Theodoxus fluviatilis is a small but colorful European nerite that is kept by some aquarium snail fanciers. Photo: L. Wischnath.

other freshwater snails. Because these snails are hermaphroditic and can be self-fertilizing, it takes few specimens to start a colony. They lay a few eggs at a time encased in usually elongate jelly masses. The young develop rapidly and may be mature in three or four months, sometimes less. Over the next few months before they die each may lay several hundred or a few thousand eggs, so these snails are capable of extreme population explosions in an aquarium if let alone.

Like many other freshwater snails, pond snails do not survive well at higher temperatures, ceasing to feed on the vegetation, algae, and detritus and dying in a few weeks. All are short-lived anyway, making them poor investments as pets, though they are easy to culture at room temperature if you need snails to feed fishes or herps. Many can carry dangerous worms, so some caution is advised when handling them or the water in which they have been kept. No particular species is sold in the pet shops, but several types, generally brown, 10mm to 20mm snails, appear as contaminants in water plants. The species of this family are virtually impossible to identify, as might be told by the presence of over 1100 names for probably fewer than 100 valid species in the family.

RAMSHORNS

The Planorbidae is a large and complicated family of mostly tiny, disc-like air-breathing snails that are notorious as carriers of parasitic worms. With few exceptions they have red bodies because they carry hemoglobin, the same pigment and oxygen-carrier that makes mammalian

The Red Ramshorn, *Helisoma nigricans*, is a rather small, flattened, bright red snail that often is imported from South America for the aquarium trade. Photo: U. Werner.

blood red. Their shells are very depressed, usually with a sunken spire, and the animal is twisted so that it is sinistral. However, in some species the shell is also twisted so it appears normal or dextral, a situation that is hard to explain and even harder to understand when trying to orient a shell. Like their relatives the pond snails, they are hermaphroditic and thus may build up large populations quickly. They are most famous as carriers of schistosomiasis, but some are common in the aquarium hobby.

The Red Ramshorn, usually identified as *Helisoma nigricans* from South America, often is available. This 25-mm snail is

Above: View of the foot of the Red Ramshorn. Below: Developing eggs of *Helisoma nigricans* in their gelatinous case. The eggs at the left are about three days old, those at the right about seven days old. Photos: U. Werner.

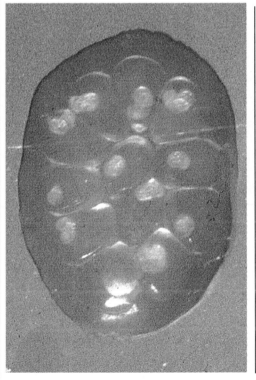

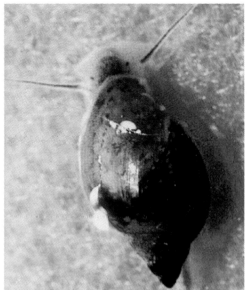

Tadpole snails such as this *Physella* species from New Jersey are often seen as contaminants of elodea and other aquatic plants. Though small and not colorful, they are easy to keep, reproduce extremely rapidly (an egg mass is show at upper left), and make great food for many fishes and even some lizards. Most species have sinistral (reversed) shells. The pair in the bottom photo appear to be mating; though hermaphroditic, cross-fertilization seems to be necessary for successful egg production. Photos: M. & J. Walls.

flattened and tightly curled, with long, slender tentacles. The animal is bright red from hemoglobin, while the shell tends to be a translucent brown. This snail is a scavenger, feeding on any organic matter it stumbles across, making it a good tank cleaner when filters cannot be used (as in fry tanks). It will eat fish eggs, however.

The European literature often mentions a ramshorn called *Planorbis corneus*, but that appears to be a cool-water Old World species that is smaller than the Red Ramshorn currently in the hobby. Many large and small planorbids enter the aquarium along with plants and sometimes fishes, and it is basically impossible to identify them with any certainty. Many species are native to the United States, including some large and rather heavy shells that might make interesting aquarium animals. Remember that all the snails of this family are potential carriers of parasites, and always take precautions when handling them and their water.

PHYSIDAE

The little physid or tadpole snails often are seen on the glass of aquaria with bunches of elodea and other soft plants. They are best treated as plant contaminants rather than snails that an aquarist would voluntarily purchase and keep, but they are

A shell of the European ramshorn *Planorbis corneus*, a popular species among European hobbyists but too sensitive to warm temperatures to maintain in the average aquarium. Photo: L. E. Perkins.

interesting. The shell is small, usually under 20mm long, slender, with a typically rather pointed spire and a large mouth. The shell is thin and crushes easily in the fingers. Their outstanding character is that physids are sinistral snails, their mouths on the left side rather than the right when you look at them through the glass side of the aquarium. Air-breathers, they are hermaphroditic and lay their eggs in gelatinous clusters. The commonly seen forms can be placed in *Physa, Physella,* or closely related genera; the more interesting genus *Aplexa* is elongate, narrow, and has a smooth, almost greasy texture. The family occurs only north of the Equator.

THIARIDS

The three species of the family Thiaridae found in the aquarium hobby often are called Malaysian live-bearing snails. They are all about 20mm to 40mm high, slender, conical, with high, pointed spires and a short body whorl and mouth. They are unusual in that all are parthenogenetic, no males being recorded. The snails hold the fertile eggs in a brood pouch in the neck, releasing fully developed female young. The edge of the

Red-rimmed Melanias, *Melanoides tuberculata*, are recognizable by the vertical reddish bands on the upper shell. This and related species often occur in tremendous numbers in the sand of aquaria and help keep the bottom clean. Large numbers can be a nuisance, however. Photo: M. Chvojka.

Red-rimmed Melanias are almost born pregnant. All are females (they are parthenogenetic) and produce fertile eggs whenever good food and habitat are present. The eggs are kept in a brood pouch until they hatch as well-developed young (female) snails. Large numbers can be produced in an aquarium from a single specimen in a matter of weeks. Photos: M. Chvojka.

mantle has finger-like projections, a feature also found in some physid snails. The species are very heavily sculptured with ridges and fine knobs, making them tiny objects of beauty when observed closely. Hobbyists use the snails to keep the bottom clean and aerated, because these snails are burrowers that are always on the move through the substrate, feeding on detritus of all types. They dislike the light so are active mostly at night or when the tank lights are turned off. Incredible numbers can occur in small areas, with 10,000 being found in a single square meter of the St. Johns River, Florida.

Thiara granifera, the Quilted Melania, has flattened sides to the whorls, compared to the more rounded whorls of *Melanoides* species. *T. granifera* is brown, without pattern, and is covered with rows of distinct little knobs; it does not reach 30mm in length. This may be the most attractive of all the aquarium snails, though it is too small to be appreciated by most hobbyists. The Red-rimmed Melania, *Melanoides tuberculata*, is the other common member of the family. It reaches about 36mm in height and has reddish flames and spots on a brown shell, along with a broad reddish brown band around the base of the shell. The sculpture (use a hand lens) consists of fine spiral threads and curved vertical ribs, the ribs most prominent on the

The Great Pond Snail, *Radix auricularia*, is a large (over 5 cm), showy but not colorful species native to northern Europe and Asia. The large size and broadly flared shell make it popular with European aquarists, but it cannot survive in warm water. Photo: M. Chvojka.

The cercaria (a type of larva) of a *Paragonimus* fluke. Melanias serve as intermediate hosts for such flukes, which occasionally may be transferred to human hosts. As always, caution is advised when handling specimens of wild snails and changing their water. Art: J. R. Quinn.

middle and upper whorls of the shell and in juveniles. The Faune Melania, *M. turricula*, is very similar but lacks the reddish band at the base of the shell and also lacks most of the curved vertical ribs except on the upper (younger) spire whorls; it may be a variety of the Red-rimmed Melania. All three species are introduced into Florida and are likely to occur in any ponds where fishes and plants are raised, so any of the three may occur in pet shops. They serve as intermediate hosts for the human lung fluke, *Paragonimus westermanni*, a dangerous parasite.

A fairly typical pond snail, *Lymnaea stagnalis*. This and similar species often are found in pet shop aquaria with aquatic plants. Notice the flattened, triangular tentacles (below) typical of the family and a good recognition character. Photos: M. Chvojka.

NERITES

The last group of snails we'll mention are the nerites, mostly marine or brackish water species that are seldom seen by the freshwater hobbyist. They are solid shells with low or depressed spires and a generally oval shape. The operculum is thick and has a pair of pegs that lock it into position to help conserve water during low tide periods. The European *Theodoxus fluviatilis* is a small snail (under 10mm high and 15mm wide) found in cool, flowing, heavily vegetated waters, a habitat now rare in Europe, making the little snail even more desirable to European hobbyists. The sexes are separate, and the female lays many small clusters of eggs in jelly capsules. Only one egg from each capsule develops, but the snails mature fast and reproduce quickly. They can tolerate only cool water, preferably under 82°F (28°C). Their blackish to yellowish shells are marked with white flecks, spots, zigzags, and other markings so that no two individuals are alike in coloration.

In the southern United States is found the attractive brackish water *Neritina reclivata*, the Olive Nerite, a species that sometimes enters the hobby as a freshwater snail. The shell is thick, glossy, and about 20mm high and wide; the green background color usually is covered with numerous fine vertical black stripes, and the

Nerites are mostly marine species, but some are well adapted to very low salinity brackish waters. This Brazilian *Neritina* is typical of the group, though some are more colorful. Photo: M. & J. Walls.

Neritina reclivata, the Olive Nerite, is an abundant little snail of warm brackish waters around the Caribbean and Gulf of Mexico. It occasionally is found in shipments of fishes from Florida and can be adapted to freshwater aquaria if you are patient and slowly reduce the salt content of the water over a few weeks. Photo: M. & J. Walls.

mouth area is glossy white. Similar species occur in brackish waters of the tropical Caribbean and Central America and might be adaptable to aquaria. Like other nerites, it feeds by scraping diatoms and other fine algae from hard surfaces and the stems of plants.

SNAIL ERADICATION

You will never have to worry about a population explosion of apple snails, of course, but the small pond snails, ramshorns, and melanias can reproduce at a tremendous rate and literally overrun an aquarium if neglected. Various chemicals, such as copper sulfate, will kill snails, but they also will damage other invertebrates and may affect the plants (including the bacteria in the filter). More complex chemicals are sold as snail eradicators, but they tend to be expensive, often dangerous to use, and not always effective on the melanias.

Hand-picking snails works well in many cases, especially if they are baited into a small bottle or net. Melanias can be collected in large numbers by turning off the lights for a day or two so the snails come out onto the aquarium glass.

The most satisfactory way to get rid of snails is to use tropical fishes. There are many suitable fishes for the purpose, including

APPENDIX

A COUPLE OF APPLE SNAIL RECIPES

Though not traditional fare in North America or Europe, apple snails are a common item on the menu in Latin American and Oriental countries. They are a readily available protein source that is cheap and tasty. Snails are pulled from the shell with a hook or tweezers after being lightly boiled or frozen to kill the animal. Only the foot is eaten, the rest of the body (including the internal organs and the operculum) being discarded. Usually the foot is chopped into small pieces or passed through a grinder.

Because apple snails may carry dangerous parasites, they should never be eaten raw or poorly cooked. In some countries it is traditional to pickle apple snails in a vinegar and pepper mixture, but this does not always kill parasites unless several weeks or even months pass. Raw chopped apple snails added to salads (similar to bacon bits in the United States) are especially dangerous. ALWAYS THOROUGHLY COOK ANY APPLE SNAILS PREPARED TO BE EATEN.

The following two recipes may serve as inspiration if you wish to be especially adventurous or happen to have an excess of snails. They are not recommended for the diet-conscious, especially the croquettes.

APPLE SNAILS IN WHITE WINE

Ingredients:

2 cups apple snail, chopped	6 cloves garlic
1 tablespoon lemon	2 teaspoons oregano
2 teaspoons pepper	2 chopped sweet peppers
2 cups tomato sauce	1 cup white wine
1 cup water	1 sliced onion
1 teaspoon salt	2 tablespoons olive oil

Simmer the apple snails in an uncovered skillet in olive oil with the garlic, lemon, oregano, pepper, salt, sweet pepper, and tomato sauce. Add the white wine, water, and sliced onion. Cover the skillet and cook for 20 minutes. Serve with rice or potatoes. Serves six.

APPLE SNAIL CROQUETTES

Ingredients:

2 cups apple snail, chopped	1 cup enriched flour
1 tablespoon grated onion	1 cup milk
1 tablespoon lemon juice	1 teaspoon salt
1 teaspoon pepper	2 eggs
2 tablespoons tomato sauce	1 cup fine bread crumbs
1 tablespoon chopped parsley	4 pounds butter
1 cup frying oil	

Cook the apple snails in a covered skillet for 30 minutes or until the meat softens, using 1 tablespoon frying oil with onion, tomato sauce, pepper, and lemon juice added.

Melt 4 pounds of butter and blend with the flour and salt. Gradually stir in milk and cook until the mixture thickens. Cook over low heat for 5 minutes and cool. Stir in the apple snails and parsley until completely mixed. Mold the mixture into croquette form and dip in bread crumbs, then in beaten eggs, and again in bread crumbs. Fry in hot oil until brown. Serves six.

GLOSSARY

Ampullariid: A member of the snail family Ampullariidae.

Angulated: Having an angled rather than a rounded contour.

Aperture: The opening or mouth of a snail through which the body emerges; it marks the anterior end of a snail shell.

Apex: The posterior tip of a snail's shell.

Apical: Situated at or close to the apex.

Body whorl: The last complete whorl of the gastropod. It usually is the largest whorl and encloses the foot and most of the rest of the snail's body.

Canaliculate: Bearing a groove or channel.

Carinate: Having one or more sharp spiral ridges or edges on the outer shell surface.

Class: Taxonomic category between phylum and order.

Columella: The internal column around which the whorls revolve.

Compressed: A spire that is relatively flattened from side to side.

Concentric: Progressively larger circles originating from the same center, as in the operculum.

Convex: Bulging or rounding outward.

Corneous: Horn-like in texture.

Cusps: The cutting blades that project from a radular tooth.

Depressed: A spire that is flattened dorso-ventrally.

Dextral: Coiled clockwise. To determine if a shell is dextral, hold it with the aperture toward you; if the aperture is on your right, it is dextral. See sinistral.

Dioecious: Having separate sexes.

Discoidal: Round and flat like a disk.

Dorsal: The back or upper side; the side opposite to the aperture.

Early whorls: The first or embryonic whorl of the shell spiral.

Elevated: Raised or lengthened.

Elongate: Referring to shells or spires when they are higher than wide.

Family: Taxonomic group of genera with common characteristics. The names of families end in -idae.

Foot: The muscular ventral part of the body of snails that serves mainly for locomotion.

Gastropoda: The snails. Class of mollusk characterized by a single-valved shell that usually coils around a central axis (the columella). The largest group of living mollusks, containing terrestrial, freshwater, and marine members.

Genus: A group of related species.

Globose: Globular or spherical.

Growth lines: Minute lines evident on the shell surface, formed during each growing period.

Hipostracum: Innermost part of the shell that is directly in contact with the animal. It is formed of calcium carbonate and has a nacreous or porcellaneous aspect.

Imperforate: Lacking an umbilicus.

Lateral teeth: Teeth located to

each side of the central tooth of the radula.

Lip: Edge of the aperture of a shell.

Malacology: The science that studies mollusks.

Malleated: Dented as if hit by a hammer.

Mantle: The skin covering the viscera of mollusks.

Marginal teeth: Teeth located at the edge of the rows of the radula.

Multispiral: An operculum with numerous slowly enlarging spirals from a single point.

Nuchal lobes: Lobes located on both sides of the body behind the eyes; one becomes the siphon.

Nucleus: The first formed part of a shell or operculum.

Oblique: Greater or less than a right angle.

Operculum: A corneous or calcareous plate borne on the dorso-posterior part of the foot in prosobranch snails that closes the aperture when the animal is retracted inside and protects it from adverse conditions.

Ostracum: The intermediate layer of a shell; formed of calcium carbonate.

Oval: Refers to shells or opercula with one end narrower than the other.

Oviparous: Laying eggs.

Patelliform: Shaped like an obtuse cone; limpet-like.

Paucispiral: An operculum with rapidly enlarging spirals from a single point.

Perforate: A shell having an umbilicus.

Periostracum: Thin layer of proteinaceous material covering most molluscan shells.

Periphery: The edges of a shell as seen in outline.

Planispiral: A shell coiled in one plane.

Prosobranch: Subclass of snails characterized by having an operculum and usually breathing by means of gills.

Pulmonate: A group (subclass) of snails lacking an operculum and usually breathing with a lung-like organ.

Radula: A rasp-like structure located in the anterior end of the digestive tract of mollusks (except bivalves), used to scrape food during feeding. It is formed by a number of longitudinal and transverse rows of teeth that have one or more cusps.

Rounded: Shells with more or less curved whorl outlines.

Sculpture: Natural markings on the surface of a shell.

Shoulder: Projecting outer peripheral part of a whorl of a shell.

Spiral: Winding, coiling, or circling around a central axis.

Spire: The whorls of a snail shell other than the body whorl.

Subglobose: Nearly globular or spherical in shape.

Suture: The line on the shell surface where two adjoining whorls meet.

Umbilicus: An opening or cavity at the base of the shell of a snail. The cavity is formed in the shell where the inner sides of the coiled whorls do not join.

Whorl: One complete turn or coil of the shell of a snail.

BIBLIOGRAPHY

The following bibliography refers mainly to the apple snails, but we have included a few references to other snails of aquarium interest.

Alderson, E. G. 1925. *Studies in Ampullaria.* Heffer & Sons: Cambridge.

Bequaert, J. C. 1957. Biological investigations in the Selva Lacandona, Chiapas, Mexico. *Bull. Mus. Comp. Zool., Harvard,* 116: 204-207.

Boss, K. J. 1982. Mollusca. Pages 945-1166, In: Parker, S. P. *Synopsis and Classification of Living Organisms.* McGraw-Hill: New York.

Brown, D. S. 1980. *Freshwater Snails of Africa and Their Medical Importance.* Taylor & Francis, Ltd.; London. 487pp.

Brunner, G. 1971. Danger at a snail's pace: Be wary of aquatic snails. *Trop. Fish Hobbyist,* 20(2): 80/93.

Burch, J. B. 1989. *North American Freshwater Snails.* Malacological Publ.; Hamburg, Michigan. 365pp.

Burch, J. B. 1991. Glossary of North American freshwater malacology. I. Gastropoda. *Walkerana,* 5: 263-288.

Cazzaniga, N. 1987. *Pomacea canaliculata* (Lamarck, 1801) en Catamarca (Argentina) y un comentario sobre *Ampullaria catamarcensis* Sowerby, 1874 (Gastropoda: Ampullariidae). *Iheringia, Serie Zoologica, Porto Alegre,* 66: 43-68.

Cazzaniga, N. 1990. Sexual dimorphism in *Pomacea canaliculata* (Gastropoda: Ampullariidae). *Veliger,* 33: 384-388.

Cazzaniga, N. & A. Estebenet. 1984. Revision y notas sobre los habitos alimentairos de los ampullaridae (Gastropoda). *Historia Natural,* 4: 213-224.

Cazzaniga, N. & A. Estebenet. 1985. Revision de antecedentes sobre el uso de caracoles acuaticos (Ampullariidae) en programas de contral biologico. *Malezas,* 13: 23-39.

Cazzaniga, N. & A. Estebenet. 1990. A sinistral *Pomacea canaliculata* (Gastropoda: Ampullariidae). *Malacological Review,* 23: 99-102.

Cowie, R. H. 1993(1995). Identity, distribution and impacts of introduced Ampullariidae and Viviparidae in the Hawaiian Islands. *J. Med. & Appl. Malacol.,* 5: 8 pp.

Crowley, T. E. & T. Pain. 1964. A monographic revision of the Mollusca of Lake Nyasa. *Ann. Mus. R. de l'Afr. Cent. (Sci. Zool.),* 131: 1-58.

Dall, W. H. 1904. Notes on the genus *Ampullaria. J. Conch.,* 11: 50-55.

Demian, E. S. & A. M. Ibrahim. 1972. Sexual dimorphism and sex ratio in the snail *Marisa cornuarietis* (L.). *Bull. Zool. Soc. Egypt,* 24: 52-63.

Estebenet, A. & N. Cazzaniga. 1993. Egg variability and the reproductive strategy of *Pomacea canaliculata* (Gastropoda: Ampullariidae). *Apex,* 8: 129-138.

Ferrer, J. R., G. Perera & M. Yong. 1991. Growth, mortality and reproduction of *Pomacea paludosa* (Say) in natural conditions. *Proc. 10th International Malacological Congress (Tubingen, 1989)*: 379-382.

Ferrer, J. R., H. Mone, G. Perera & M. Yong. 1991. Rol de *Marisa cornuarietis* como agente de control biologico y sus implicaciones economicas y epidemiologicas. *Revista Cubana Medicina Tropical*, 43: 31-35.

Hylton Scott, M. I. 1957. Estudio morfologico y taxonomico de los ampullaridos de la Republica Argentina. *Revista argent. Cienc. nat. Bernardino Rivadavia Inst. nac. Invest. Cienc. nat., Cienc. Zool.*, 3: 233-333.

Jokinen, E. H. 1983. The freshwater snails of Connecticut. *Bull. State Geol. & Nat. Hist. Surv. of Conn.*, No. 109: 1-83.

Jutting, W. S. S. v. B. 1956. Critical revision of the Javanese freshwater gastropods. *Treubia*, 23: 259-477.

Keawjam, R. 1986. The apple snails of Thailand: Distribution, habitats and shell morphology. *Malacological Review*, 19: 61-81.

Keawjam, R. 1986. Laboratory maintenance, narcotization and induction of aestivation of apple snails (Mesogastropoda: Pilidae). *Malacological Review*, 19: 111-112.

Keawjam, R. 1987. Guide for the identification of freshwater snails of the family Pilidae in Thailand. *Walkerana*, 8: 173-186.

Kobelt, W. 1911-15. Die gattung *Ampullaria*. In: Martini & Chemnitz, *Syst. Conch.-Cab.*

Leloup, E. 1953. *Exploration Hydrobiologique du Lac Tanganyika*, 3(4). Tervuren.

Lopes, H. S. 1955. Sobre duas especies do genero *Pomacea* Perry com un estudo da genitalia em ambos os sexos (Mesogastropoda, Architaenioglossa, Mollusca). *Revista Brasileira Biologia*, 15: 203-210.

Mandahl-Barth, G. 1954. The freshwater molluscs of Uganda and adjacent territories. *Ann. Mus. R. du Congo Belge (Sci. Zool.)*, 32: 38-49.

Masters, C. O. 1981. Live-bearing snails. *Trop. Fish Hobbyist*, 30(3): 86-87.

Masters, C. O. 1984. The great pond snail. *Trop. Fish Hobbyist*, 32(11): 85-86.

Michelson, E. H. 1961. On the generic limits in the family Pilidae (Prosobranchia: Mollusca). *Breviora (MCZ)*, No. 133: 1-10.

Naranjo, E. 1986. Algunas consideraciones sobre el genero *Pomacea* (Gastropoda: Pilidae) en Mexico y Centroamerica. *Anales del Instituto de Biologia Universidad Autonoma Mexico*, 56: 603-606.

Pain, T. 1950. *Pomacea* (Ampullariidae) of British Guiana. *Proc. Malac. Soc. London*, 28: 63-74.

Pain, T. 1960. *Pomacea* (Ampullariidae) of the Amazon

River system. *J. Conch.*, 24: 421-432.

Pain, T. 1961. Revision of the African Ampullariidae. Species of the genus *Pila* Roding, 1798. *Ann. Mus. R. de l'Afr. Cent. (Sci. Zool.)*, 96: 1-27.

Pain, T. 1964. The *Pomacea flagellata* complex in Central America. *J. Conch.*, 25: 224-231.

Pain, T. 1972. The Ampullariidae, an historical survey. *J. Conch.*, 27: 453-462.

Pain, R. & S. Arias. 1958. Descripcion de una especie nueva de *Pomacea* de Venezuela (Mesogastropoda, Architaeniglossa, Mollusca). *Novedades Cientificas. Contribuciones ocasionales del Museo de Historia Natural de La Salle*, 24: 5-11.

Paraense, W. L. 1981. Gastropoda. In: *Aquatic Biota of Tropical South America*. San Diego State Univ.; San Diego, CA. 298pp.

Perera, G. & J. P. Pointier. 1995. Ampullarid snails: Forgotten creatures of the freshwater world. *Trop. Fish Hobbyist*, 43(10): 234-242.

Perera, G., J. P. Pointier, M. Yong & J. R. Ferrer. 1991. Comparacion del crecimiento de 2 especies de *Pomacea* de la region antillana utiles como agentes de control de enfermedades tropicales. *Revista Cubana Medicina Tropical*, 43: 36-38.

Perera, G. & M. Yong. 1991. Seasonal studies on *Pomacea paludosa* in Cuba. *Walkerana*, 5: 19-23.

Petrovicky, I. 1968. Snails and the aquarium. *Trop. Fish Hobbyist*, 16(9): 36/53.

Pilsbry, H. 1927. Revision of the Ampullariidae of Jamaica and Cuba. *Proc. Acad. Nat. Sci. Philadelphia*, 79: 247-253.

Pilsbry, H. 1933. Zoological results of the Matto Grosso Expedition to Brazil in 1931.-II. Mollusca. *Proc. Acad. Nat. Sci. Philadelphia*, 85: 67-76.

Pilsbry, H. & J. Bequaert. 1927. The aquatic mollusks of the Belgian Congo, with a geographical and ecological account of Congo malacology. *Bull. Amer. Mus. Nat. Hist.*, 53: 69-602.

Ponder, W. F. & A. Waren. 1988. Classification of the Caenogastropoda and Heterostropha—a list of the family-group names and higher taxa. *Malacol. Rev.*, Suppl. 4: 288-326.

Rangel Ruiz, L. J. 1988. Estudio morfologico de *Pomacea flagellata* Say, 1827 (Gastropoda: Ampullariidae) y algunas consideraciones sobre su taxonomica y distribucion geografica en Mexico. *Anales Instituto Biologia de la Universidad Nacional Autonoma de Mexico*, 58: 21-34.

Sowerby, G. B. III. 1909. Notes on the family Ampullariidae, with a list of species, varieties, and synonyms, also descriptions of four new species. *Proc. Malac. Soc. London*, 8:345-364. Also: 9: 56-64; 12: 65-73.

Starmuhlner, F. 1989. The alluring apple snails. *Trop. Fish Hobbyist*, 37(5): 52/57.

Thiengo, S. C. 1987. Observations on the morphology of *Pomacea lineata* (Spix, 1827) (Mollusca: Ampullariidae). *Memorias do Instituto Oswaldo Cruz*, 82: 563-570.

Thiengo, S. C. 1989. On *Pomacea sordida* (Swainson, 1823) (Prosobranchia: Ampullariidae). *Memorias do Instituto Oswaldo Cruz*, 84: 351-355.

Thiengo, S. C., C. E. Borda & J. L. Barros Araujo. 1993. On *Pomacea canaliculata* (Lamarck, 1822) (Mollusca: Pilidae: Ampullariidae). *Memorias do Instituto Oswaldo Cruz*, 88: 67-71.

Thompson, F. G. 1984. *The Freshwater Snails of Florida*. Univ. Presses Florida: Gainesville, FL. 91pp.

Tillier, S. 1980. Gasteropodes terrestres et fluviatiles de Guyane Francaise. *Mem. Mus. d'Hist. nat.*, 118: 16-33.

Vargas, M., J. Gomez & G. Perera. 1991. Geographic expansion of *Marisa cornuarietis* and *Tarebia granifera* in the Dominican Republic. *J. Med. and Appl. Malacol*, 3: 69-72.

Werner, U. 1983. Snails for the aquarium. *Trop. Fish Hobbyist*, 32(1): 8/12.

Wischnath, L. 1989. So splendid a snail: *Theodoxus fluviatilis*. *Trop. Fish Hobbyist*, 38(3): 34/38.

Yong, M. 1991. Se atreveria Ud. a comer *Pomacea? Noticiario de la Sociedad Espanola de Malacologia*, 12: 32-34.

PHOTO INDEX

TEXT INDEX

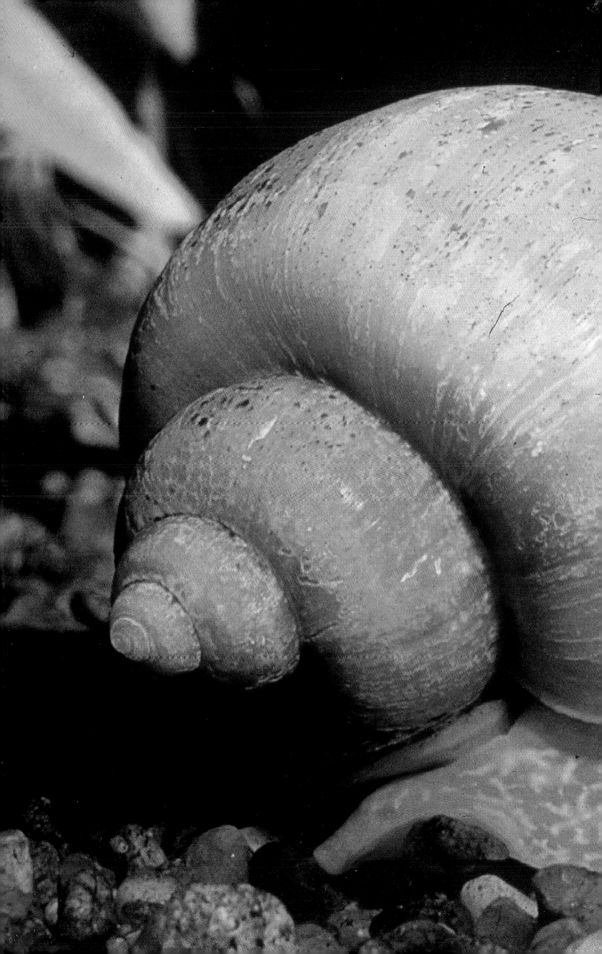